FAUNA

AUSTRALIA'S MOST CURIOUS CREATURES

FOR LEXI, WITH LOVE—GREAT AUNTIE TAN x

THANK YOU

Fauna would not have been possible without my fabulous publisher Susan Hall, designer extraordinaire Amy Cullen, image editor Stephanie Morris, and scientific editor Jeanette Birtles, whose expertise and advice was enormously appreciated. Thanks, also, to the people who make animals and faunal conservation part of their life's work. Our world is richer for it, and my research would have been impossible without you.

Published by National Library of Australia Publishing
Canberra ACT 2600

ISBN: 9780642279767

First published 2019, reprinted 2020. Paperback edition published 2021, reprinted 2023, 2024, 2025.

The National Library of Australia acknowledges Australia's First Nations Peoples—the First Australians—as the Traditional Owners and Custodians of this land and gives respect to the Elders—past and present—and through them to all Australian Aboriginal and Torres Strait Islander people.

Commissioning Publisher: Susan Hall
Editor: Jeanette Birtles
Graphic designer: Tania McCartney
Production designer: Amy Cullen
Image coordinator: Stephanie Morris
Printed in China by Asia Pacific Offset

The National Library of Australia would like to thank Janet Wilson for her help with this book.

Find out more about NLA Publishing, including teachers' notes, at nla.gov.au/national-library-publishing.

A catalogue record for this book is available from the National Library of Australia

FAUNA

AUSTRALIA'S MOST CURIOUS CREATURES

TANIA McCARTNEY

Australia is one of only 17 'megadiverse' countries, which together contain more than two-thirds of the world's plant and animal biodiversity. It is home to more animal species than any other developed country, and a whopping 87 per cent of our mammals, 45 per cent of our birds, 93 per cent of our reptiles and 94 per cent of our amphibians are found nowhere else on earth.

Because of the way these animals have evolved on our isolated island nation, they have become some of the most unusual and most curious of creatures. But how well do we know our beloved native curiosities? *Fauna* explores just some of these unique additions to our rich faunal landscape.

The animals in this book have been introduced in random order—much as we would discover them in our natural environment.

At the end of the book, you'll find a family tree that shows how these animals fit in with the rest of the animal kingdom. Zoologists have been dividing animals into these scientific groups for a very long time, and they continue to discover both similarities and differences between the animals we all know and love, and those creatures only recently discovered.

The following markers appear alongside many of the animals in this book, indicating their current conservation status.

LET'S EXPLORE OUR CURIOUS CREATURES!

EX – EXTINCT
EW – EXTINCT IN THE WILD
CR – CRITICALLY ENDANGERED
EN – ENDANGERED
VU – VULNERABLE
NT – NEAR THREATENED
LC – LEAST CONCERN

CONTENTS

THE KOALA

(*Phascolarctos cinereus*)

TEDDY BEAR?

Australia's own teddy bear, the koala is not really a bear. It's an arboreal, nocturnal, herbivorous marsupial—or in other words, a fluffy, tree-dwelling leaf-eater with a pouch, who sleeps all day and wakes briefly at night. Its closest living relative is the wombat!

STATE SPECIES

There are three subspecies of koala. The Queensland koala is the smallest, with short, silver fur. The Victorian koala is the largest, with shaggier, brown fur, and the New South Wales koala falls somewhere between the two. Victorian koalas are actually twice as heavy as Queensland koalas.

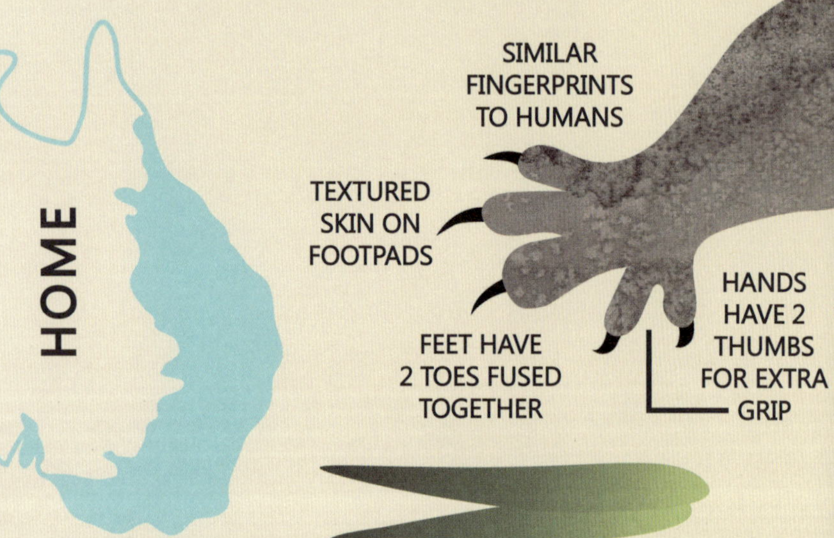

YOU'VE GOT TO HAVE FRIENDS

Koalas prefer to spend time alone, though the mother–joey bond is very strong. Adult males communicate with loud bellows. Grunts and bellows are also made while mating and can be heard kilometres away!

BELLOW!!!

TREE CAMEL

'Koala' comes from an Indigenous word meaning 'no drink'. Koalas rarely need water, as gum leaves are so high in water content.

DROP BEARS

The drop bear is a predatory, carnivorous koala. It is large and vicious and will drop from trees onto the heads of unsuspecting people below (though if you speak with an Australian accent, you may be safe). Okay, they're actually imaginary creatures. **OR ARE THEY?**

JOEYS

ACTUAL SIZE AT BIRTH

A newborn joey is tiny and undeveloped, and about the size of a jelly bean. The baby (and sometimes a twin) crawls into its mother's upside-down pouch, which is closed off with a sphincter muscle so the baby can't fall out. At around 6 months, a little fluffball pokes its head out of the pouch. When the baby is ready to leave the pouch, the mother eats leaves and produces a pap that the joey licks from her bottom **EWWWW!** . . . but it's not poop! It's full of bacteria to help the baby digest leaves.

NOSH TIME

Koalas eat about a kilo of leaves each day, and prefer the leaves of certain types of eucalypt. The leaves are low in nutrition and are high in fibre and toxins! A special part of their digestive system (called a caecum, pronounced see-kum) helps koalas digest the leaves and also process the toxins. This digestive process is so exhausting, they will sleep up to 20 hours a day. Koalas can store leaves in their cheek pouches before chewing them, and they'll occasionally eat the flowers, buds, twigs and bark of eucalypts, as well as a little dirt. Only a certain number of koalas can live in one forest because a lack of leaves can starve the population and make it sick.

WELL-DEVELOPED MIDDLE EAR FOR GOOD BALANCE

UP TO 85cm HIGH

ONE OF THE SMALLEST BRAINS (FOR ITS SIZE) OF ANY MAMMAL

A VERY GOOD SENSE OF SMELL

EXTRA BRAIN FLUID THAT MAY ACT AS A SHOCK ABSORBER, IN CASE OF FALLS

EYES ARE SMALL AND THE PUPILS ARE VERTICAL SLITS

INSULATING, WATERPROOF FUR, RESISTANT TO SUN, WIND AND RAIN

A PAD AT THE BASE OF THE SPINE FOR COMFORT

A GROUP OF KOALAS IS CALLED A **COLONY**

VU

80,000?

ON THE BRINK

One of the biggest threats to koalas is Chlamydiaceae bacteria, which leads to eye, urinary and reproductive tract infections. Drought, bushfires, dogs, humans and loss of habitat are also responsible for the koala's rapid population decline. The koala is now listed as vulnerable, and the Australian Koala Foundation estimates there are fewer than 80,000 koalas left in the wild.

TERRITORY WARS

The male koala has chest glands that he rubs against trees to mark his territory. He may also wee on tree trunks!

TAKE A DIP

Koalas are very good swimmers, though as gum leaves don't provide much energy, they do tire easily. They will sometimes swim—to cross creeks or just to cool down.

THE CROCODILE

(*Crocodylus*)

LC

TOP OF THE FOOD CHAIN

The largest of all living reptiles, the crocodile's closest relatives are birds and dinosaurs. The saltwater croc (*Crocodylus porosus*) is nicknamed the 'saltie'. It can grow up to 6.2 metres in length and weigh as much as 1,000 kilograms. It lives in estuaries, lagoons and freshwater rivers, and can even wander out to sea. Salties usually live 50 to 60 years, and they are considered the most dangerous animal in Australia. During the Mesozoic Era, around 100 million years ago, the Crocodilia order was one of the top animal groups in the food chain. It still is.

Its bite pressure is the strongest of any living animal, yet, amazingly, the muscles that open the croc's mouth are so weak, its snout can be kept closed with a rubber band (don't try this at home!).

9cm

CHOMP CHOMP

Salties have up to 66 teeth, with the largest growing as long as 9 centimetres. The teeth are quickly replaced—a croc can go through a whopping 8,000 teeth in a lifetime.

SUNBATHING

Generally lazy, crocs love to bask in the sun during the day, and will hunt at night. They can't sweat, so they open their mouth to cool down . . . a bit like a dog panting.

A GROUP OF CROCODILES IS CALLED A **BASK**

WIDE SNOUT

TRANSPARENT EYELIDS

EXCELLENT SIGHT, SMELL AND HEARING

SMALL BRAIN

POWERFUL JAW

SMALL FRONT LEGS

WEBBED FEET

HOME

0cm

FRESHWATER CROC

The freshwater crocodile (*Crocodylus johnstoni*) inhabits inland rivers and lagoons. Its range sometimes overlaps with that of saltwater crocs. Freshies are half the size of salties, growing up to 3 metres long. They eat smaller prey such as fish, turtles, frogs, snakes, water birds, and even insects!

THE HUNTER

Salties are aggressive hunters—much more so than freshwater crocs. Most prey are ambushed and drowned by the 'death roll', then either swallowed whole or torn into chunks. Hiding in the water, with only their nostrils and eyes above the surface, salties can lie motionless for long periods of time. They can also stay fully submerged for up to 2 hours by reducing their heart rate to just a few beats per minute. Crocs occasionally eat stones to help break down food. They can actually go for months without food, and generally eat a full meal only once a week. The larger the croc grows, the more varied its diet. Prey include fish, shellfish, mammals and birds, even those as large as emus and magpie geese.

CROCODILE TEARS

Salties 'cry' when they eat, because gulping their food means they swallow a lot of air. This stimulates their tear glands. Boo hoo!

3 TIMES FASTER THAN HUMANS IN THE WATER!

SUBMERGED

Crocs spend up to 11 hours a day in the water. When they dive, their nostrils shut and their throat is closed off by a large flap of skin. Special glands on the tongue eliminate extra salt from the body, allowing them to thrive in salt water.

CROC NURSERY

The female croc lays an average of 50 eggs in a sandbar, on a riverbank or swamp, and she will lurk near the nest for the full 3-month incubation period. Amazingly, the nest temperature is responsible for gender. Below 30ºC, babies will be female. Between 30 and 32ºC, they will be male. At 33ºC or higher, the hatchlings will be mostly female. When ready to emerge, the babies cry out from inside the mound and the mother digs them out, carrying them to the water in her mouth. Newly hatched salties measure around 29cm, and only 1 per cent survive to adulthood, with 99 per cent being eaten by predators. No wonder Mum gets a little cranky!

ACTUAL EGG SIZE 8cm

A TOUGH, BUMPY HIDE IS CAUSED BY BONY PLATES (OSTEODERMS) UNDER THE SKIN

MUSCULAR TAIL, FLATTENED ON BOTH SIDES

SOFTER BELLY SKIN

STRONG BACK LEGS

ACTUAL HATCHLING SIZE

ADULTS CAN GROW LONGER THAN A GIRAFFE IS TALL

29cm

THE LYREBIRD

(Menura novaehollandiae + Menura alberti)

SOUND BITE BIRD

A bird that chirps like a chainsaw, chatters like a camera shutter and screeches like a car alarm? The superb lyrebird is Australia's third-largest songbird and our finest mimic. This ancient bird dates back 15 million years, but today there are just two species—the superb lyrebird (*Menura novaehollandiae*) and Albert's lyrebird (*Menura alberti*), named in honour of Queen Victoria's husband. Albert's lyrebird lacks the elegant lyre-shaped tail feathers of the male superb lyrebird. It's also a little smaller, and is now only found in a tiny pocket of Southern Queensland rainforest.

HELLO!
CLANG CLANG!
WAAAAAAA!
BANG!
WOOF WOOF!
RING RING!

LYRE LYRE

The ornate tail of the superb lyrebird male is up to 70cm long and takes 7 years to develop. The two outermost feathers make the shape of a lyre.

MASTER MIMICS

The lyrebird's syrinx (voice organ) is the most complex of all songbirds, giving it extraordinary vocal ability. It has a beautiful singing voice—and will often sing for hours each day—but what's best known about this bird is its remarkable ability to perfectly mimic the calls of other birds and even other animals (like koalas). The lyrebird can imitate almost any sound—a car alarm, a rifle shot, a mobile phone, a dog barking, a baby crying, and even the human voice.

SHAKE YOUR TAIL FEATHER

Female lyrebirds are plain, but the male is kind of fancy, and uses both elaborate plumage and dramatic rituals to attract females. First, he builds several mounds of dirt to use as platforms, then he'll sing his heart out from dawn to dusk for as long as 6 weeks. He's not very choosy, and will mate with every female he attracts. The Albert's lyrebird uses a more modest pile of small twigs for his platform. During courtship, both types of male throw their tails forward and shake their backsides, shimmering the canopy of feathers above their heads.

THE NEST DOME

When she's ready to lay, the female builds a messy, dome-shaped nest of sticks, twigs and leaves, lined with her own feathers. She incubates a single egg and then raises the downy white chick for up to 10 weeks. Chicks will screech loudly if an intruder enters the nest.

STRONG SENSE OF SMELL

SHORT, ROUNDED WINGS, INCAPABLE OF FLIGHT

STRONG FEET + LONG CLAWS

SUPERB: 103cm

ALBERT'S: 90cm

0cm

SUPERB: LC

ALBERT'S: NT

WHAT'S IN A NAME

Early names given to the lyrebird include native pheasant, peacock-wren and bird-of-paradise.

COLOURWAYS

Lyrebird feathers vary through browns, tans and greys, and can even have little pops of colour. This Albert's lyrebird has a flush of bright orange and blue on its head, neck and tail feathers.

SCRATCHING FOR DINNER

Lyrebirds scratch and forage all day long for insects, worms, spiders, frogs and other small creatures. Their foraging speeds up the decay of forest litter, reducing fuel for forest fires.

THE SUPERB LYREBIRD LIVES UP TO 19 YEARS

A GROUP OF LYREBIRDS IS CALLED A MUSKET

HOME

- Superb
- Albert's

ON THE MONEY

The superb lyrebird is featured on the reverse side of the Australian 10 cent coin.

HOME SWEET HOME

Lyrebirds prefer rainforest habitat and a dense understorey of vines and shrubs. They roost in trees at night.

SEA DWELLERS

Australia has some of the most varied and dangerous sea dwellers on the planet, and our marine environments teem with 4,000 different types of fish. One hundred million years ago, the centre of Australia was covered in water. The Eromanga Sea thronged with life, including fierce marine dinosaurs like the Australian ichthyosaur.

PHOTOSYNTHETIC SEA SLUGS

(Order: Sacoglossa)

Found in shallow coastal waters, sacoglossan sea slugs look more like crawling seaweed than animals. Known as 'sap-sucking sea slugs' (try saying that fast!), they 'steal' chloroplasts from seaweed and store them in their digestive tract (turning the slug bright green). Incredibly, this solar-powered slug uses these chloroplasts to draw energy from the sun—by the process of photosynthesis—for as long as 9 months!

JELLYFISH HAVE BEEN AROUND FOR 600 MILLION YEARS

BOX JELLYFISH

(*Chironex fleckeri*)

The Australian box jellyfish is the world's most venomous animal. A single jellyfish can have enough poison to kill 60 adults, and the venom can be fatal within 5 minutes. Its tentacles grow up to 3 metres long and release microscopic darts containing venom. Being almost transparent, the box jellyish can be difficult for swimmers to see and avoid. They have 4 eye clusters, with a total of 24 inward-facing eyes. It's unknown how they use these eyes, as they have no central nervous system.

BLUE-RINGED OCTOPUS

(*Hapalochlaena*)

Found in tidal pools of Pacific Ocean coastlines, these tiny creatures range from 4 to 6cm in body (or 'mantle') length, with arms from 7 to 10cm long. They are one of the world's most venomous animals, and there can be enough venom in one bite to kill 26 adults. Usually blending in with its surroundings, the octopus turns bright yellow when disturbed, and its blue rings flash iridescent blue. It has three hearts and blue blood.

TOTALLY WEIRD

A cookiecutter shark? A faceless fish? A herd of sea pigs and a meat-eating sponge? These totally weird creatures might just be too freaky for this book! Look them up online, and be amazed and astounded.

ANGLERFISH (Antennariidae)
SEA SPIDER (Pycnogonida)
COOKIECUTTER SHARK (*Isistius brasiliensis*)
SEA PIG (*Scotoplanes*)
CARNIVOROUS SPONGE (*Cladorhiza*)
ZOMBIE WORM (*Osedax*)
FACELESS FISH (*Typhlonus nasus*)
TRIPOD FISH (*Bathypterois grallator*)
CROWN-OF-THORNS STARFISH (*Acanthaster planci*)
TASMANIAN GIANT CRAB (*Pseudocarcinus gigas*)

MORE WEIRD CREATURES ARE BEING DISCOVERED ALL THE TIME

THE POISON TETRODOTOXIN IS 100 TIMES MORE TOXIC THAN CYANIDE!

BLOWFISH

(Torquigener pleurogramma)

The blowfish gets its name from its ability to puff up with water when threatened. If taken from the water, it will puff up with air instead—the ultimate fish balloon! The blowfish helps keep waterways clean by gobbling up rotting matter like bait or burley. They are one of the most poisonous vertebrates in the world, containing a lethal poison called tetrodotoxin. Curiously, larger fish won't die when they do manage to gobble a blowfish.

WOBBEGONG

(Family: Orectolobidae)

Meaning 'shaggy beard' in an Indigenous language, wobbegongs have seaweed-like whiskers called 'barbels' around their noses. With 12 species in total, these bottom-dwelling fish have elaborate patterning, which explains why they're also called 'carpet sharks'. Unlike other sharks, which need to move to breathe, wobbegongs can stay motionless, using their cheeks to pump water through their gills. They can walk across the ocean floor on their bottom fins and can even cross land, from one tidal pool to another. When you eat fish and chips, you may be eating wobbegong.

YELLOW-BELLIED SEA SNAKE

(Hydrophis platurus)

The most wide-ranging snake in the world, this highly toxic species travels vast distances and is capable of great bursts of speed. It swims by undulating its body, both forwards and backwards. On land, the snake is unable to stay upright, and this it why it never leaves the water. Because it also avoids the sea floor, the snake has no hard objects to rub against when shedding skin. Instead, it ties itself in a knot, coiling and twisting to loosen old skin.

VENOMOUS ANIMALS BITE, STING OR INJECT POISON

POISONOUS ANIMALS HAVE TO BE BITTEN OR TOUCHED TO HAVE AN EFFECT

BLOBFISH

(Psychrolutes marcidus)

More like a blob of slime than a fish, this curious creature features a distinctive nose and a wide, clown-like mouth. As the fish has no gas bladder to keep it afloat, its gelatinous body allows it to hover just above the ocean floor, reaching depths many other fish can't. With very few hard bones and little muscle, the blobfish was once voted the world's ugliest animal. Maybe you think he's kind of cute?

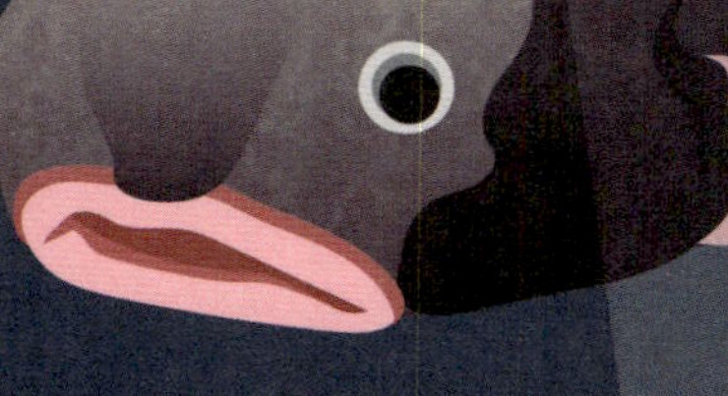

THE KANGAROO

(*Macropus*)

THE GANGURRU

The word kangaroo comes from the Guugu Yimithirr word 'gangurru'. These large marsupials were described by early explorers as having heads like deer, standing upright like men and hopping like frogs (as well as occasionally 'two-headed', when females have a joey in the pouch!). The kangaroo is the largest macropod (meaning 'big foot'). Its ancestor—the giant kangaroo—can be traced back 20 million years to north-western Queensland.

HOME

Roos live practically everywhere!

LC

LONG, MUSCULAR TAIL USED FOR HOPPING, BALANCE, AND AS A FIFTH LIMB

JOEY JELLY BEANS

At birth, the joey is the size of a jelly bean. It climbs into its mother's pouch where it will feed on milk, emerging in about 9 months. Joeys go to the toilet in their mum's pouch! Much of it is absorbed, but mum will occasionally lick the pouch clean. Eastern grey roos can 'freeze' the development of embryos (which is called 'embryonic diapause') and can have three babies on the go at once. When the female's pouch becomes free of a joey, the next baby will be born and a fertilised egg will start developing into a new embryo. Amazingly, the female is able to produce two different kinds of milk at the same time—one for a newborn and one for an older joey.

POWERFUL BACK LEGS

ON THE HOP

Kangaroos are the only large animals to use hopping to get around, often covering vast distances. The leg tendons act like springs, allowing them to move fast and in a highly energy-efficient way. Kangaroos can't walk backwards, and they often use their tail as a fifth leg.

ROOS CAN BOUND AS HIGH AS 3m

PART OF THE MOB

Kangaroos roam, rest and feed in groups from as small as a handful to several hundred. They groom each other and also protect each other by stomping their feet on the ground when a predator is near. They communicate using a series of clucking sounds and, if upset, guttural coughs.

COOL IT

Roos can't sweat. They cool down by licking their fur, and may also swim. Some species are crepuscular (grazing during cooler mornings and evenings) and others are nocturnal (grazing at night).

ALL IN THE FAMILY

There are four species of large kangaroo. Wallabies and wallaroos are smaller types of roo, and other relations include pademelons, potoroos, bettongs, rat-kangaroos, tree-kangaroos and quokkas.

2m
1m
0m

ANTILOPINE

Macropus antilopinus is the smallest, and is the far-northern equivalent of the eastern and western greys.

WESTERN GREY

Macropus fuliginosus is a little larger, and is found in South Australia, southern Western Australia, and the Darling River basin.

EASTERN GREY

Macropus giganteus is the second largest. It lives in the fertile east of the country, including eastern Tasmania.

RED

Macropus rufus is the largest surviving marsupial in the world. It lives in the arid centre of Australia. The tallest ever recorded reached 2.4 metres!

EARS CAN ROTATE 180°

324° VISION (HUMANS HAVE 180°)

THE EASTERN GREY IS FASTEST AT 65 km/h

ALMOST NO VOCAL CHORDS

SMALL FORELIMBS

POUCH

LARGE HIND FEET

A GROUP OF ROOS IS CALLED A MOB

THE FEEDBAG

Kangaroos are herbivores, eating grass, flowers, leaves and moss. Their front teeth crop grass and their back molars grind it. When the molars have been ground down, they will fall out and be replaced with new teeth that grow from the back. The only other mammals to do this are elephants and manatees. Roos have two stomach chambers. They regurgitate their food, chew it and then swallow it again, a bit like cows do.

MOOOO!

THEY CAN LEAP AS FAR AS 13m

THE WESTERN GREY SMELLS LIKE CURRY!

THE BOXING KANGAROO

Male roos fight by rising onto their hind legs and tail, and 'boxing' each other. They also lock forearms and wrestle. Inspired by travelling sideshows where men fought roos with boxing gloves, the boxing kangaroo first appeared in a cartoon in 1891. During the Second World War, the boxing roo was painted onto the sides of Australian aircraft. It's now a symbol of Australian sport.

THE PLATYPUS

(*Ornithorhynchus anatinus*)

IS IT A BIRD?

This extraordinary creature is a living connection to our earliest mammals of 166 million years ago—laying eggs like a reptile or bird, but covered in fur and suckling its young like a mammal. The platypus astonished early settlers in Australia, and many people back in England thought it was fake. The platypus and the four echidna species are the only living monotremes.

MONO-HUH?

The platypus is a monotreme—a mammal that lays eggs. The female lays between 1 and 3 eggs (mostly 2), which are incubated in a burrow for around 10 days. The babies emerge blind, hairless and the size of a jelly bean. The mother has no pouch; instead, she cradles the babies between her body and tail. Her milk leaks through her belly skin, and the babies suck it from her fur. They do this for 3 to 4 months before leaving the burrow to forage for food on their own. A baby platypus can swim as soon as it is weaned.

ACTUAL EGG SIZE

MONSTERPUS

Fossils have revealed a prehistoric ancestor of the platypus, around 1 metre long and with ferocious teeth. Scientists have dubbed it 'Platypus Godzilla'. Today, adult males measure up to 64cm from bill to tail, and babies are born with tiny teeth that they actually lose in adulthood. The platypus is no longer a monster, but is still intriguing!

LC

YEOWCH!

The male has a venomous spike on his back leg. Although not deadly to humans, the venom is said to cause excruciating pain.

DIGGING DEEP

There are two types of platypus burrow—one for nesting and one used for 'camping' out of the water, and as a safe house. The platypus uses its claws to dig several burrows that are just big enough for 1 or 2 occupants. The female digs a much deeper burrow for nesting.

TADPOLES

BEETLES

HIGH-TECH MEALS

Electroreceptors are built into the bill of the platypus, allowing it to detect food as it swims.

FROGS

LOTS OF PLATYPUS

The plural for platypus is 'platypuses' or just 'platypus' (like 'sheep'). Some people call them 'platypi', which sounds like Latin but isn't. In Greek, where the word originates, it would actually be 'platypodes'.

A GROUP OF PLATYPUS IS CALLED A **PADDLE**

BELLY ACHE

Over millions of years of evolution, the stomach of the platypus disappeared! Of all vertebrate animals (those with a backbone), only fish and monotremes have no stomach.

ON THE HUNT

The ears and eyes of the platypus sit in a muscular channel that pinches shut when it dives under water. Its nostrils also close, and it uses its sensitive bill to find and scoop up food, along with sand and gravel. It stores this in its cheeks, then floats on top of the water to eat its stash. Because it has no teeth, the gravel helps the platypus grind its food. The platypus eats no plants at all!

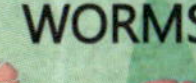

INSECT LARVAE

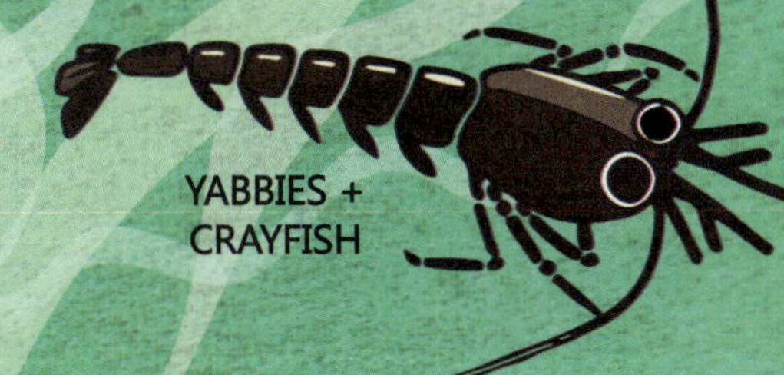

TAIL

VENOMOUS SPIKE (MALES)

CLAWS + RETRACTABLE WEBBING

PARTIALLY WEBBED FEET

WEBBED FEET

THICK FUR

EARS

EYES

NOSTRILS

BILL

DEEP DIVER

The platypus can stay under water for up to 10 minutes, and it can forage for an astonishing 16 to 18 hours a day.

IT CAN EAT THE EQUIVALENT OF ITS BODY WEIGHT IN JUST 24 HOURS

THE HOAX

Indigenous Australians knew better, but European settlers thought the platypus was fake and had been cobbled together from the body parts of other animals!

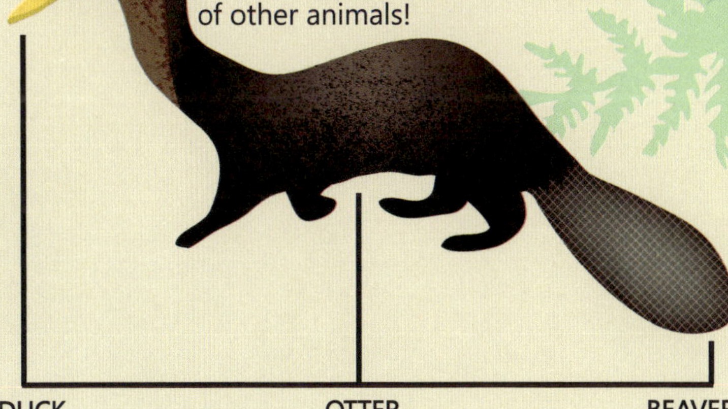

THE CASSOWARY

(Casuarius casuarius johnsonii)

A MODERN DINOSAUR

Resembling an oversized prehistoric turkey on stilts, the southern cassowary is one of three types of cassowary, and the only one to be found in Australia. It can weigh as much as 80 kilograms and can grow as tall as 2 metres, making it the third-tallest and second-heaviest bird in the world. With scaly legs, quill-like feathers, head casque and strange colouring, its appearance has been likened to the Jurassic velociraptor.

EN

NINJA BIRD

This astonishing bird can run as fast as 50km/h, jump as high as 2 metres, and swim long distances. Because its feathers aren't waterproof, the cassowary shakes itself like a dog after a swim.

EXCEPTIONAL HEARING AND EYESIGHT

HELMET HEAD

The casque sits on top of the head and has a sponge-like centre, covered in keratin (like your fingernails). Each bird has its own uniquely shaped and coloured casque, which begins forming around age 2. Scientists aren't sure of the casque's function. Is it a tool? A weapon? A transmitter and receiver? A protective helmet? Or just a fancy headdress?

WARNING!

The cassowary is considered the most dangerous bird in the world. Normally reclusive and shy, it can become aggressive if threatened. It first hisses a warning. Then, if further provoked, the bird can charge and kick, slashing its dagger-like claws through the air.

FEATHERS ARE LONG, FINE AND ALMOST HAIR-LIKE. THERE ARE NO WING OR TAIL FEATHERS AT ALL

CLOSE-UP

TONGUELESS

The cassowary has no tongue, so food must be thrown back into the throat to swallow it. Water is scooped up with the lower beak.

HEAD AND NECK CHANGE COLOUR, DEPENDING ON MOOD

HOME

The cassowary is confined to two pockets in far north Queensland.

THERE ARE ONLY AROUND 1,200 BIRDS LEFT IN THE WILD

A GROUP OF CASSOWARIES IS CALLED A MOB BUT ALSO A DASH, JUMP, RUN OR SLASH!

ELEPHANT CALL

Grunting more like an elephant than a bird, the southern cassowary has one of the lowest frequency calls of any bird in the world. It can reach as low as 24 hertz, which only just sneaks into the human hearing range. Sounds include grunting, rumbling, clacking, burping, hissing and booming.

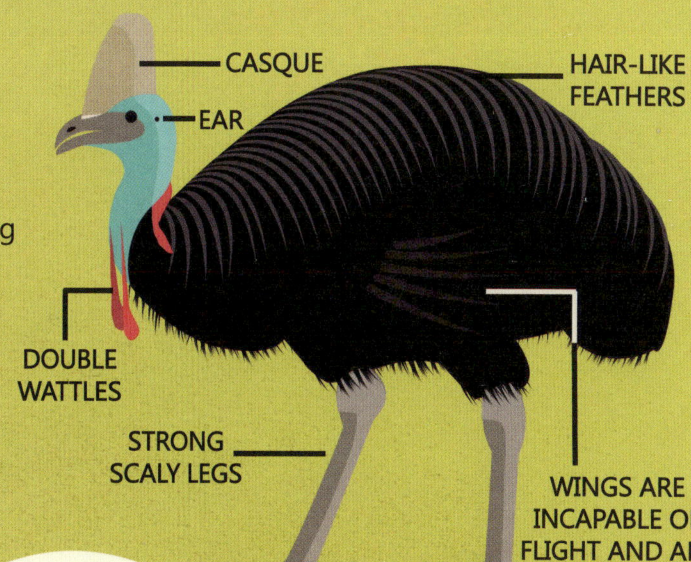

ECO-POOP

The cassowary eats fruit whole, and seeds pass through the digestive tract untouched. As the bird wanders the rainforest, its seed-laden 'scats' help reseed almost 100 types of plants (23 of these actually rely on processing by the cassowary's digestive system), making the bird a vital part of the rainforest ecosystem. You could say that cassowary scat is some of the most ecological poop on the planet!

ACTUAL EGG SIZE

DADDY DAY-CARE

The female lays 3 to 5 bright green or blue eggs in a nest made by the male. Dad then sits on the eggs for the next 50 days and refuses to leave, not even for food or to pee! When the chicks hatch, he looks after them on his own, teaching them how to survive. When they are ready to leave home, Dad chases the chicks away!

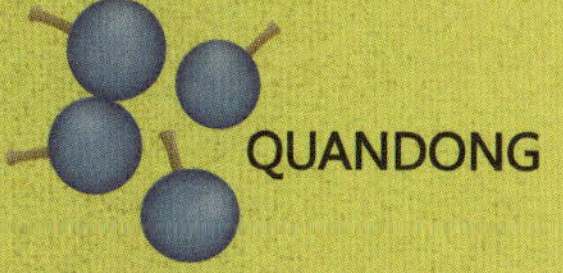

BROWN WALNUT FRUIT

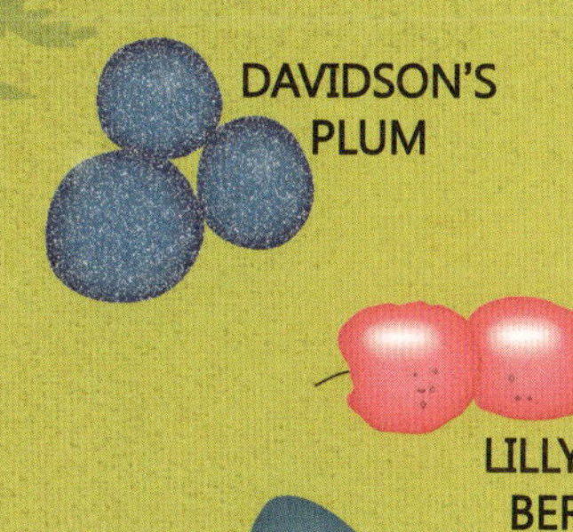

FRUIT SALAD

The cassowary is a frugivore, existing mainly on fruit, and it simply adores the cassowary plum, which is toxic to humans and most other animals. Its short digestive tract and specialised stomach acid make short work of these toxins. The bird sometimes supplements its diet with leaves, fungus, frogs, insects, snakes and other small animals.

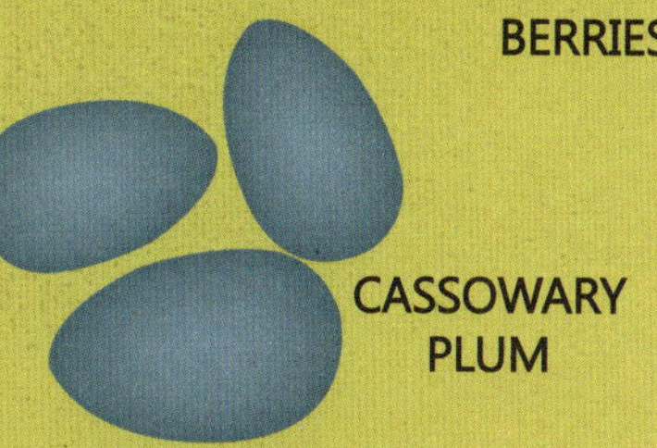

INVERTEBRATES

SPINELESS WONDERS

It's estimated that Australia has up to 300,000 land invertebrate species, but only 160,000 have been named or described. They play a critical role in maintaining biodiversity, and without them, the world wouldn't last long at all. Indigenous Australians relied on these animals for nutrition, with favourites being the bogong moth, witchetty grub (which tastes like almonds!) and honeypot ant. Invertebrates and their by-products were also used as medicine, antiseptic, anaesthetic, and even as wound dressings. They were used for the arts, too. Limonite oxide, found in ants' nests, was used as a yellow pigment for painting, and objects could be sculpted from beeswax. Australia has some of the deadliest invertebrates in the world. Some invertebrates may be poisonous and scary, but spiders, for example, are actually less dangerous than snakes, sharks . . . or even bees!

EN

EASTERN TARANTULA BIRD-EATING SPIDER

(*Phlogius crassipes*) Australia's largest spider, this whopping arachnid eats insects, frogs, toads and even birds. With a leg span of 16 centimetres, it has enough venom to kill a dog. This amazing spider can bark, whistle and hiss, but usually just sticks to its burrow.

AUSTRALIAN TIGER BEETLE

(*Cicindela hudsoni*) Super speedy for its size, the tiger beetle moves faster than most adults can walk (9km/h), and if it was scaled up to human size, it would be running at 770km/h! Because it runs so fast, its eyes can't keep up. Everything blurs and it has to stop to check where its prey is!

GIANT PINK SLUG

(*Triboniophorus* aff. *graeffei*) These fluorescent pink slugs are only found on Mount Kaputar, northwest of Sydney. When a volcano erupted millions of years ago, it created a unique alpine environment for the slug. Growing up to 20 centimetres long, these striking creatures creep up trees after rain to feed on lichen and moss.

SCORPION

Found all over Australia, scorpions tend to be larger and more venomous in the north, where they can grow up to 12 centimetres long. Despite having 6 to 12 eyes, they don't have good eyesight. Scorpions devour their prey by covering it in digestive juices and then breaking it up with their jaws. Under ultraviolet light, scorpions are fluorescent, and breathing is an interesting experience—they have lungs on their bellies!

CARNIVOROUS SNAIL

(*Vitellidelos kaputarensis*) One of several species unique to Mount Kaputar, this predatory snail picks up the slime trails of vegetarian snails, tracks them down and gobbles them up!

LORD HOWE ISLAND STICK INSECT

(*Dryococelus australis*) Critically endangered, this is one of the world's rarest invertebrates, thought to have been wiped out by introduced rats in the 1920s. Rediscovered in 2001, this stick insect grows up to 12 centimetres long and is also called the tree lobster.

12cm

ACTUAL SIZE

GIANT BLUE EARTHWORM

(*Terriswalkeris terraereginae*) Resembling a rather large lolly snake, this deep blue worm of far north Queensland releases a glow-in-the-dark mucus. It grows up to 2 metres long.

VU

BE VERY AFRAID...

A 3-metre worm? A giant cockroach? A spider who moonlights as an assassin? Explore these particularly creepy critters.

GIANT GIPPSLAND EARTHWORM

(*Megascolides australis*) Found in eastern Victoria, this giant worm can grow up to 3 metres long. It's the only earthworm on our endangered list.

WHITE CEDAR MOTH CATERPILLAR

(*Leptocneria reducta*) These fuzzy critters come out at night, swarming silently up tree trunks to gobble every leaf. Watch out—their bristles can cause severe skin rashes.

GIANT CENTIPEDE

(*Ethmostigmus rubripes*) Measuring up to 16 centimetres and with 23 pairs of legs, the giant centipede is the largest in Australia. A nocturnal, venomous feeder, it's been known to feed on snakes!

GIANT BURROWING COCKROACH

(*Macropanesthia rhinoceros*) Living in burrows in northern Queensland and growing up to 8 centimetres, this is the heaviest cockroach on earth. Young cockroaches (which are born live) stay in the burrow while mum and dad feed them dry leaf litter torn into little pieces. They live up to 10 years and can be kept as pets!

PEACOCK SPIDER

(*Maratus volans*) Just like an actual peacock, the male peacock spider raises a colourful fan-like flap to attract females, vibrating its hind legs and abdomen.

ASSASSIN SPIDER

(*Austrarchaea raveni*) With enormous spear-like jaws, these spiders hang upside down on a thread and await their prey—almost always other spiders. They are survivors from the Age of Dinosaurs.

SCORPION-TAILED SPIDER

(*Arachnura higginsi*) When threatened, the female scorpion-tailed spider arches her tail as an actual scorpion would. She strings her eggs up on her web like a decorative wall hanging.

SYDNEY FUNNEL-WEB SPIDER

(*Atrax robustus*) Funnel-webs, especially the Sydney funnel-web, are the most dangerous spiders in Australia. Their fangs can pierce a toenail, and their venom can kill humans in less than 15 minutes.

CAIRNS BIRDWING BUTTERFLY

(*Ornithoptera euphorion*) Australia's largest endemic butterfly species, its wingspan can reach 15 centimetres. When feeding on flowers, it supports its weight by madly flapping its wings.

HERCULES MOTH

(*Coscinocera hercules*) The Hercules moth has the largest moth wing-span in the world (27 centimetres). When it emerges from its cocoon, it never feeds (and so doesn't live long!). The caterpillar has bright yellow spikes and markings on its backside that mimic eyes.

THE MARSUPIAL MOLE

(*Notoryctes caurinus* + *Notoryctes typhlops*)

MYSTERIOUS MOVER

Not much is known about this blind marsupial that 'swims' beneath the desert dunes and sand plains of central and western Australia. The sole genus of the Notoryctidae family, there are two types of marsupial mole—the northern (*Notoryctes caurinus*) and the southern (*Notoryctes typhlops*), which is slightly larger. Known, respectively, as the 'kakarratul' and 'itjaritjari' by local Indigenous people, they are featured in Indigenous Australian mythology. About the size of a rat, marsupial moles are considered to be perfectly crafted burrowing machines, and are very different from all other marsupials. Evidence suggests they branched off from the marsupial family tree just after dinosaurs became extinct . . . 64 MILLION YEARS AGO

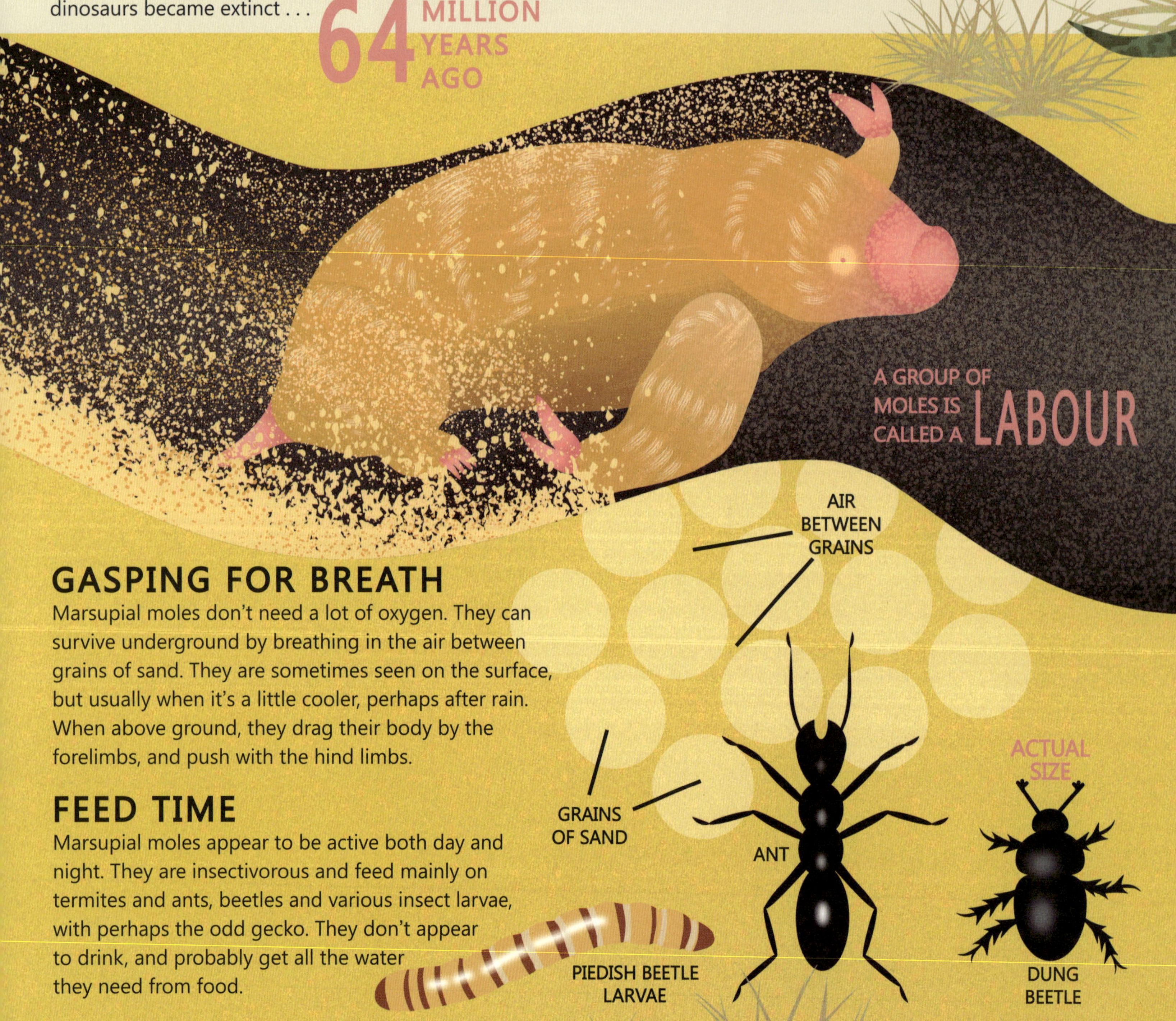

GASPING FOR BREATH

Marsupial moles don't need a lot of oxygen. They can survive underground by breathing in the air between grains of sand. They are sometimes seen on the surface, but usually when it's a little cooler, perhaps after rain. When above ground, they drag their body by the forelimbs, and push with the hind limbs.

FEED TIME

Marsupial moles appear to be active both day and night. They are insectivorous and feed mainly on termites and ants, beetles and various insect larvae, with perhaps the odd gecko. They don't appear to drink, and probably get all the water they need from food.

LITTLE DIGGERS

Marsupial moles are thought to produce one or two young. At birth, babies crawl into the backwards-facing pouch (which contains two teats). Males actually have pouches, too, though they are underdeveloped and have no teats.

TUNNELLING

A marsupial mole moves underground by burrowing along just beneath the surface, pushing against the sand with its hard, padded nose. The sand backfills the tunnel as it moves along, allowing it to 'swim' underground. Silky fur, which can be pinkish in colour, helps the mole slip through the sand more easily. Much of its burrowing is horizontal, 8 to 20 centimetres below the surface, but occasionally it will burrow vertically. It's believed to use a series of high-pitched sounds to communicate underground.

LC

HOT + COLD

An extraordinary temperature management system allows these moles to cope with extreme temperatures. Like reptiles, their metabolic rate drops very low when at rest, but can be 60 times faster when burrowing. They seem to be able to select the temperature of their environment by burrowing to different depths.

8cm – 20cm

MAY BURROW VERTICALLY AS DEEP AS

2.5m

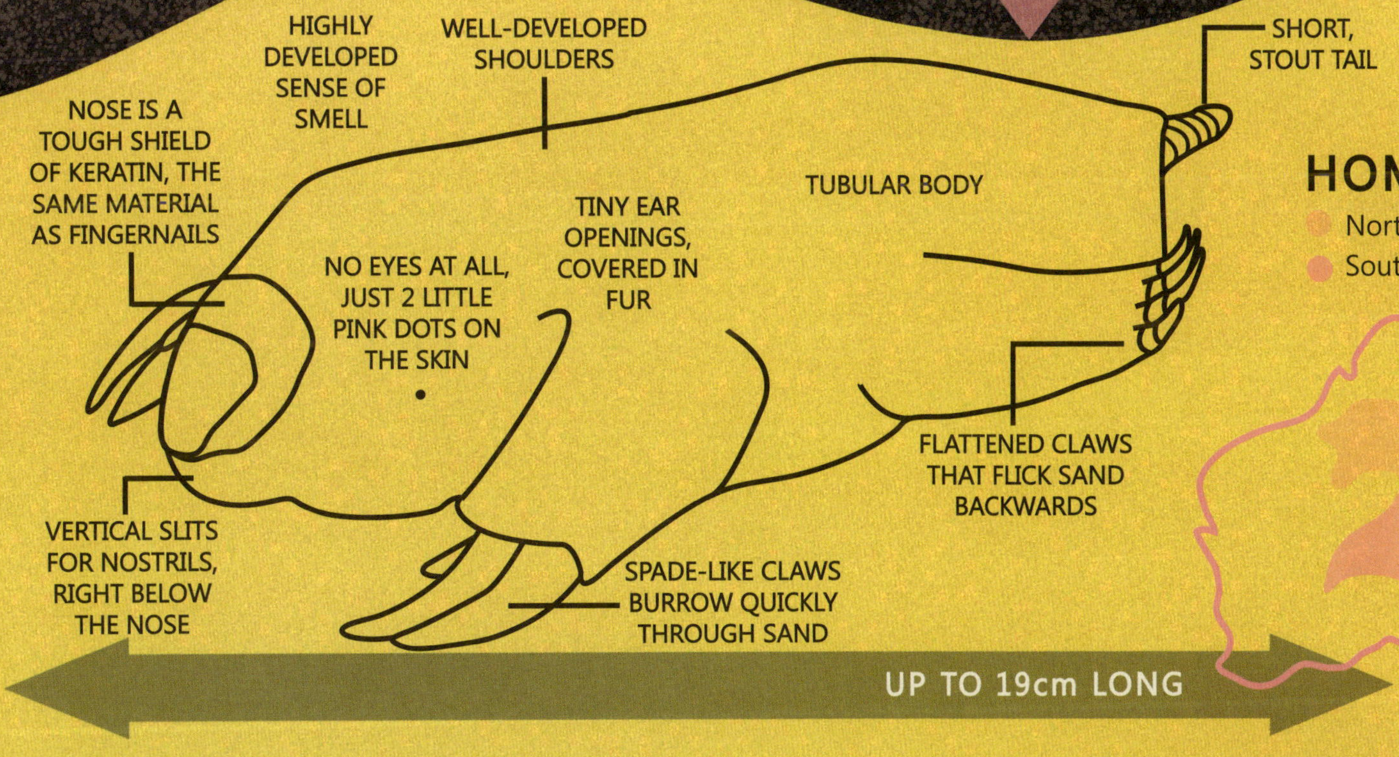

HIGHLY DEVELOPED SENSE OF SMELL

WELL-DEVELOPED SHOULDERS

SHORT, STOUT TAIL

NOSE IS A TOUGH SHIELD OF KERATIN, THE SAME MATERIAL AS FINGERNAILS

TUBULAR BODY

TINY EAR OPENINGS, COVERED IN FUR

NO EYES AT ALL, JUST 2 LITTLE PINK DOTS ON THE SKIN

VERTICAL SLITS FOR NOSTRILS, RIGHT BELOW THE NOSE

FLATTENED CLAWS THAT FLICK SAND BACKWARDS

SPADE-LIKE CLAWS BURROW QUICKLY THROUGH SAND

UP TO 19cm LONG

HOME

Northern

Southern

THE SUGAR GLIDER

(*Petaurus breviceps*)

THE FLYING SQUIRREL

It may look like a 'flying squirrel', but this little cutie is really a nocturnal, omnivorous, arboreal, gliding marsupial. This means it's active at night, eats both plants and animals, lives in trees, and can 'fly' through the trees with the greatest of ease ... even though it's a possum! The sugar glider's name comes from its ability to glide and its love of nectar, sap, tree gum and sugary lerps (the crystallised honeydew coverings of lerp insect larvae), most particularly those found on eucalypt leaves. The Australian sugar glider has been around a very long time. Earliest fossils date back 15,000 years.

SUGAR BABIES

Babies are carried in a pouch that opens upwards so little ones can't fall out. There are four teats, but the female mostly gives birth to two joeys, who nestle in the pouch for around 2 months. Young ones will ride on Mum's back until they're older. Male sugar gliders also take care of babies, and one parent will snuggle with the young to keep them warm while the other parent is out hunting food. When building a nest, gliders can use their tails to carry leaves. A grasping tail is called 'prehensile', but the sugar glider's tail is only semi-prehensile. In other words, the tail isn't strong enough to hold the glider's own weight, so you won't see it hanging by its tail.

WHAT'S FOR DESSERT?

Sugar gliders are omnivores and eat a variety of foods in addition to their sweet sap and nectar treats. Foods include insects, spiders, eggs, seeds, fungi, fruits, and even small lizards and birds. They also eat a lot of pollen, and so pollinate many species of plant when they glide about. Gliders get half of their water from rainwater, and the rest is found in their food.

BEETLES

EGGS

SPIDERS

SEEDS

POLLEN

FRUIT

FUNGI

NECTAR

THE GENUS NAME *Petaurus* ROUGHLY TRANSLATES AS

TIGHTROPE WALKER

HOME

These adorable marsupials inhabit wet and dry sclerophyll forests, rainforests, and acacia scrub in northern and eastern Australia. In 1835, the species was introduced to Tasmania.

AERIAL ACROBATS

The sugar glider doesn't actually fly. It stretches its legs out and glides on a patagium (membrane) that extends from the forefoot to the hindfoot. Able to cover distances of 50 metres or more, it uses its membrane muscles, along with body, arm and tail movement, to steer and adjust its speed. It uses gliding to move from tree to tree, to snap up food mid-air, and to avoid predators. In fact, this fuzzy little critter rarely touches the ground!

FLIGHT CLUB

Sugar gliders are very social animals, living in family groups of a dominant male and up to 6 females and their babies. The male has 4 scent glands, used for marking territory. To form close bonds, gliders groom one another, using saliva and gland scents to mark each group member. Intruders without scent markers are quickly chased away. These tiny possums also communicate through squeaks, barks, hisses, and visual signals.

SLEEPYHEADS

Sugar gliders tire easily, and in order to conserve energy they go into torpor—a sort of short hibernation. Gliding also helps them save energy.

REPTILES + AMPHIBIANS

REPTILES

Reptiles have scales, a shell or crocodile scutes (external bony plates). Nearly all reproduce by laying shelled eggs, but some give birth to live young. Australia has more species of venomous snake than any other country. They include many of the world's most venomous snakes, such as the inland taipan (perhaps the most venomous snake of all), the eastern brown snake, the coastal taipan and the tiger snake. Our reptiles are divided into three basic groups: turtles, crocodiles, and snakes and lizards.

AUSTRALIA HAS THE MOST DIVERSE RANGE OF REPTILES, AT ALMOST 1,000 SPECIES

FRILL-NECKED LIZARD

(*Chlamydosaurus kingii*) Belonging to the dragon family, the frill-necked lizard looks like an escapee from Jurassic Park. It has a pleated flap of skin around its neck that it extends when threatened, during territory disputes, when needing to cool down, or just when looking for a girlfriend! It spends much of its time in trees, but descends to feast on termites. When threatened, it opens its bright pink or yellow mouth and starts to hiss. Females lay eggs in an underground nest, and temperature determines the gender of the babies—above 35°C, all will be female. The frill-necked lizard has a hilarious way of rising onto its back legs and running along with its front legs flapping. It can lighten or darken its skin to match its environment.

SCRUB PYTHON

UP TO 7m LONG!

(*Morelia kinghorni*) Australia's largest native snake is an excellent tree climber, and it grows so big, it can eat large wallabies! Its scales give off a milky, iridescent sheen.

BURTON'S LEGLESS LIZARD

(*Lialis burtonis*) This snakelike lizard has no forelegs and only tiny flaps for hind legs. With an elongated snout and retractable eyes, it ambushes its prey. It can suffocate larger prey by holding it tight around the chest, then swallowing it whole, head first. Like other lizards, it can drop its tail if threatened.

EASTERN LONG-NECKED TURTLE

(*Chelodina longicollis*) With a half turtle/half snake appearance, this turtle tucks its long neck into its shell sideways, rather than drawing it in. Also known as a 'stinker', it can eject pungent liquid from its armpits and groin when disturbed.

COOL IT

Reptiles are 'ectothermic', which means their body temperature changes according to the temperature outside. You might know it as 'cold-blooded'.

PERENTIE LIZARD

(*Varanus giganteus*) The fourth-largest lizard on earth and the biggest in Australia, the perentie lizard grows up to 2.5 metres long. It can run as fast as 40km/h and can also swim. This giant will eat almost anything, but generally feasts on eggs, insects, carrion, other lizards, and sometimes larger animals like small kangaroos. It tracks its prey by sight and uses its long, forked tongue to pick up scents in the air. The female lays 6 to 14 eggs in a burrow or in a termite mound (where insect activity keeps them warm). If threatened, the male puffs out his throat, hisses and stands on his hind legs, clawing and lashing his tail. This lizard can dig a burrow in a matter of minutes.

AMPHIBIANS

Amphibians are ectothermic vertebrates and include frogs, toads, salamanders, newts and caecilians (snake-like amphibians). They tend to have an aquatic gill-breathing stage when young, followed by a lung-breathing adult stage. Australia has over 6,500 described amphibian species.

HIP-POCKET FROG

(*Assa darlingtoni*) This tiny frog is also called the pouched or male marsupial frog because the male has 'hip pockets', a bit like the pouches of marsupials. The female lays eggs on the ground in a glob of jelly, which are guarded by both the male and female. When the babies hatch into tadpoles, they wriggle their way into the pouches on Dad's hips. Only about half make it. Around 8 weeks later, they emerge as froglets.

TURTLE FROG

(*Myobatrachus gouldii*) This odd-looking frog resembles a turtle with no shell, having a blunt snout, beady eyes and short legs. It feeds on termites and lives in burrows underground. One of few frogs to skip the tadpole phase, babies emerge from eggs (after 6 months) as fully formed froglets. The turtle frog has one of the biggest eggs of any Australian frog species.

WATER-HOLDING FROG

(*Cyclorana platycephala*) Water-holding frogs are unique in that they can catch prey underwater, stuffing it into their mouths with their hands. During the dry season, they burrow underground, lining their burrows with mucus and shed skin. They can burrow as deep as 1 metre or more, and may stay dormant for several years. Thirsty Indigenous people dig them up, squeeze the water out, then release them unharmed.

THE ECHIDNA

(*Tachyglossus aculeatus*)

HALF MAMMAL, HALF REPTILE?

The Australian echidna is the short-beaked echidna (the long-beaked species lives in New Guinea) and there are five subspecies. The echidna and the platypus are the only surviving monotremes—the oldest living group of mammals and the only living mammals that lay eggs. Echidnas evolved around 66 million years ago, and are descended from a platypus-like monotreme. The earliest short-beaked echidna fossils date back to around 15 million years ago. Since they lay eggs, echidnas were once believed to be half mammal, half reptile. They were named after Ekhidna, a monster from Greek mythology with the head of a woman and the body of a snake.

TEMPERATURE CONTROL

The echidna can't sweat, so it avoids heat whenever it can. Its snout has a refrigerator effect, condensing water vapour in the breath and cooling it down. During winter, it will go into deep torpor or hibernation to save energy, and its body temperature can drop to as low as 5°C. Echidnas have thick hair between their spines, and in Tasmania the hair can grow so long, it almost covers the spines.

TERMITE

TOOTHLESS FEEDING

The echidna eats ants, termites and a little dirt. The dirt helps break down food, especially as the echidna has no teeth. Unlike the stomachs of other mammals, the echidna's stomach has low acid levels and is almost pH neutral. It's also elastic, and massages food to break it down.

THE NOSE KNOWS

The echidna has a strong sense of smell. Its leathery snout is keratinised and has electroreceptors that allow it to detect its surroundings, as well as prey vibrations. Its snout can't open wider than 5 millimetres but the tongue can protrude up to 18 centimetres, rapidly firing up to 100 times a minute. The tongue is stiffened by a rapid flow of blood, allowing it to penetrate soil and even wood!

THE 'BEAK' IS REALLY A LONG NOSE WITH A TINY MOUTH AND A LONG, STICKY TONGUE

NOSTRILS

TONGUE

NO TEETH

MOUTH

PUGGLES

Females makes a nursery burrow and lay just one rubbery egg a year, straight into their backwards-facing pouch. The male has no contact with the female after mating. The baby is called a puggle and is the size of a grape when born. It hatches from the egg and starts suckling from specialised patches of skin that leak milk. Puggles soon grow too large and spiky for the pouch, so move out into the nursery burrow. At 6 months, they will leave the burrow and never see Mum again.

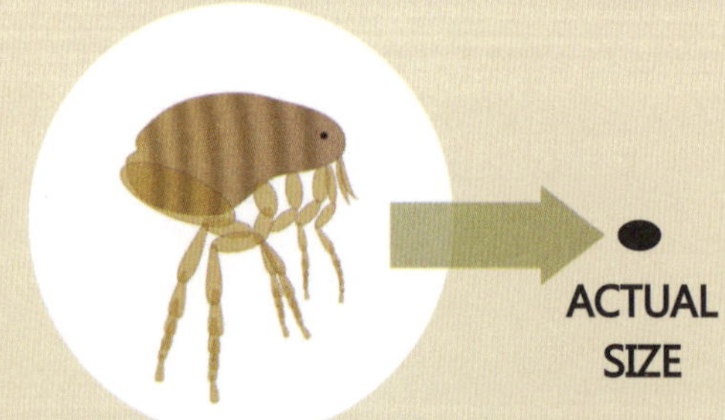

MONSTER FLEA

The echidna can carry the world's longest flea (*Bradiopsylla echidnae*), which can grow up to 4mm long.

BODY ARMOUR

When threatened, the echidna curls into a ball and presents its spines, which are made of keratin (like hair and nails). An enormous muscle that covers the entire body allows it to do this. To avoid prey, it can dig itself into the ground by using all four feet at once.

DIG IT

Excellent diggers, the echidna's strong limbs can tear apart logs and move large stones. As it spends time underground, it can tolerate high levels of carbon dioxide and low levels of oxygen. It can dig up to a metre into the ground in search of food, and can even dive underwater to survive bushfires and floods.

HOME

The echidna lives all over Australia, in all climates and terrains, making it Australia's most widespread native mammal.

A GROUP OF ECHIDNAS IS CALLED A **FLOCK**

THE LEAFY SEADRAGON

(*Phycodurus eques*)

PLANT OR ANIMAL?

Leafy seadragons are some of the most beautifully camouflaged creatures on earth. Adorned with delicate 'leaves', they blend in with seaweed and can change colour to match their surroundings. They are found in Australia's southern waters and nowhere else in the world. Although they look like elegant horses, they are actually a species of fish. Unlike most fish, their gills are small circular openings rather than crescent-shaped or ridged.

LUNCHTIME

Leafy seadragons feed on plankton, larval fish, and crustaceans like shrimp and sea lice. They suck their food through a pipe-like mouth, a bit like using a drinking straw. They have no teeth, so food is swallowed whole. Feeding, like swimming, happens at a very slow pace.

LEAFIES TRAVEL AT JUST 200m PER HOUR

HUMANS WALK AT AROUND 5km/h

ADRIFT AT SEA

Leafies are one of the few animals in the world that hide by moving. With a powerful sense of direction, they swim using a pectoral fin on their neck and a dorsal fin on their back. They can travel long distances in search of food, yet are able to find their way back to their resting location over and over again.

EASY TARGETS

These beautiful creatures face many threats. As slow swimmers, they're often eaten, and this is why camouflage is vital. They can also be washed ashore during storms, and many are stolen from the ocean by collectors or poachers (who use them in alternative medicine).

BABY DADDY

The seadragon is unusual in that the male incubates and 'gives birth' to young. The male's tail turns bright yellow when it's ready to mate, and males will fight each other to get their girl. The female deposits up to 250 bright pink eggs onto the male's tail, using a long tube. The eggs are fertilised during this transfer, and attach themselves to a 'brood patch', which has an oxygen supply. When ripe, the eggs turn orange or purple, and the male begins pumping his tail until the babies emerge. This can take up to 2 days. The young are very small and have to look after themselves.

ONLY ABOUT 5 PER CENT OF BABIES SURVIVE

CAMO

Leafies can vary in colour, from yellowy-brown to green, depending on where they live, their diet, their age, and even their stress levels!

HOME

These gentle creatures can be found in shallow waters, wherever they can be camouflaged by plants—in seaweed beds, weedy reefs and seagrass meadows.

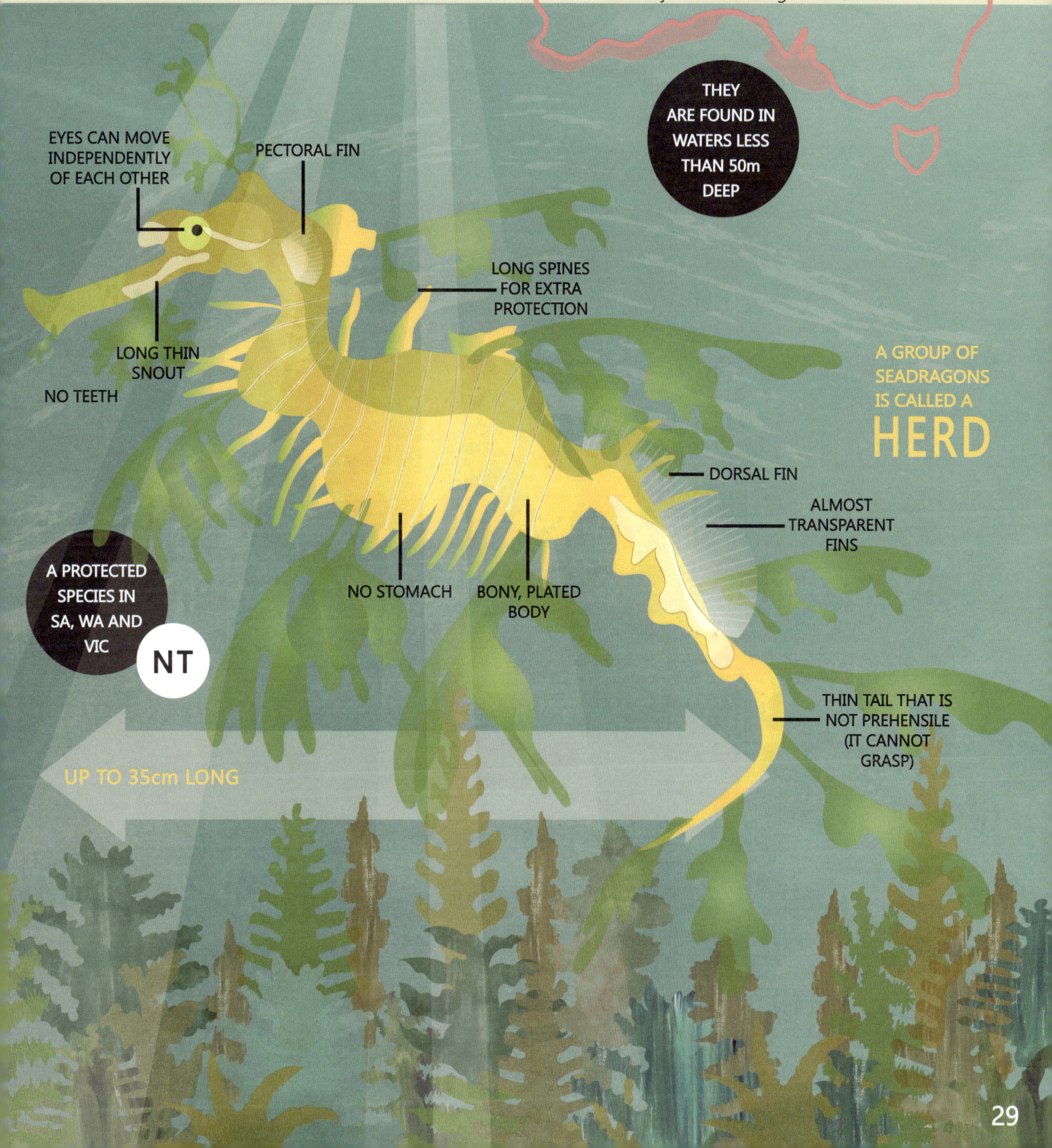

THEY ARE FOUND IN WATERS LESS THAN 50m DEEP

EYES CAN MOVE INDEPENDENTLY OF EACH OTHER

PECTORAL FIN

LONG SPINES FOR EXTRA PROTECTION

LONG THIN SNOUT

NO TEETH

A GROUP OF SEADRAGONS IS CALLED A HERD

DORSAL FIN

ALMOST TRANSPARENT FINS

A PROTECTED SPECIES IN SA, WA AND VIC

NT

NO STOMACH

BONY, PLATED BODY

THIN TAIL THAT IS NOT PREHENSILE (IT CANNOT GRASP)

UP TO 35cm LONG

BIRDS

Australia and its offshore islands and territories have around 900 recorded bird species, and over 45 per cent are found nowhere else on earth. Birds can be divided into passerine (able to perch and sing) and non-passerine. Some of our birds date back to Gondwana time—the emu, the cassowary and many species of parrot. Many are endemic to Australasia (certain swallows, thrushes, raptors), while others have been more recently introduced (such as blackbirds and sparrows). Migratory birds (like sandpipers and plovers) invite themselves to our shores, and seabirds like gulls and albatrosses come and go as they please.

LAUGHING KOOKABURRA

(*Dacelo novaeguineae*) This kookaburra is the largest kingfisher, and is probably our best-known bird. Its laugh is the sound of Australia. When one bird throws back its head, others will quickly join in, and if a rival tribe replies, the bushland soon fills with laughter. This is a great way for tribes to make their territories clear. Kookas have strong family ties. Both parents and their 'helpers' (usually older kids) incubate eggs and feed the chicks.

TAWNY FROGMOUTH

(*Podargus strigoides*) If you hear a soft, continuous 'oom oom' at night, it may be a tawny frogmouth, not an owl. In fact, the bird is often mistaken for an owl. When threatened, it freezes, pulls in its feathers and closes its eyes, resembling a broken tree branch! Nocturnal, it gobbles insects, worms, slugs and snails, as well as small mammals, reptiles, frogs, and other birds. During daylight hours, it doesn't actively hunt, but may sit with its mouth open, hoping an insect will crawl inside.

NIGHT PARROT

(*Pezoporus occidentalis*) One of the most elusive and mysterious birds in the world, the night parrot was considered extinct from 1912 to 1979, and it is now listed as endangered. Since 1979, sightings have been few, and its numbers are currently unknown. Well suited to outback life, it emerges from spinifex after sunset to forage for food. The night parrot appears to need little water.

AUSTRALIAN MAGPIE

(*Cracticus tibicen*) The magpie has an array of beautiful, complex calls, including musical warbling, with pitch varying over four octaves. It can mimic dozens of other bird species, dogs, and even human voices. The magpie is the only member of its bird family to move on the ground by walking (rather than hopping). A small percentage of magpies can become aggressive during the breeding season, swooping and clacking their beaks at animals or humans who venture near the nest. Poor cyclists seem to be attacked most.

BROLGA

(*Grus rubicunda*) Brolgas live in close family units in saltwater marshes. Their intricate mating dance begins with one bird tossing and catching grass in its beak. It then leaps up with wings outstretched, and bows, struts and calls, bobbing its head up and down. Sometimes, just one brolga dances, but they can dance in pairs or even as a group, in lines opposite one another. These large birds have to run a long way before take-off, flapping their wings madly as they lift awkwardly into the sky.

EMU

(*Dromaius novaehollandiae*) Emus are the second-largest birds in the world and the tallest in Australia. They have powerful legs and their claws can rip through wire fences! Although they can't fly, emus can swim, and can run as fast as 50km/h. They barely drink, and will eat glass, metal and stones to help grind up their food. Emus could be described as vain birds . . . they spend a lot of time preening.

VICTORIA'S RIFLEBIRD

(*Ptiloris victoriae*) The riflebird is known for its elaborate mating display. The male begins by calling, then throws his wings in upward curves, dashing his head from side to side like a wind-up toy. When a female approaches, his call becomes softer and more musical. They then face each other . . . the male claps his wings rapidly, then gives her a cuddle. Awww!

MALLEEFOWL

(*Leipoa ocellata*) The nest of the malleefowl is enormous—often 1.5 metres high and up to 4 metres wide. The male digs a hole and fills it with leaves, sticks and bark, then turns it to encourage decay. When the compost heats up, the female lays her eggs, and the male uses his beak as a thermometer to make sure the temperature is just right (34°C), adjusting the compost as necessary. Despite such loving care, the moment chicks hatch and dig their way out of the nest, both parents abandon them. Luckily, chicks can run within an hour and fly within a day of hatching.

SATIN BOWERBIRD

(*Ptilonorhynchus violaceus*) The male satin bowerbird builds special structures called bowers, made of sticks and decorated with flowers, berries, and collected items like bottle caps, pen lids and pegs. He prefers blue items, especially those that reflect ultraviolet light. The bird then paints the bower walls with chewed-up vegetation. Females will choose the male with the most impressive bower. He will also dance to win her over, giving her a blue object. After mating, the female builds a nest in a tree or bush and incubates the eggs. Both males and females have violet-blue eyes.

THE TASMANIAN DEVIL

(Sarcophilus harrisii)

CARNIVOROUS MARSUPIAL

The Tassie devil became the largest carnivorous marsupial in the world when the Tasmanian tiger (thylacine) died out in 1936. Its spine-chilling snarls and high-pitched screeches led early European settlers to call it the devil, Beelzebub's pup, satanic meatlover and bear devil. Found only in Tasmania (with a conservation project of devils on Maria Island), this aggressive marsupial is actually quite shy. Although mostly nocturnal, it's also active in the daytime.

A GROUP OF DEVILS IS CALLED A **COLONY**

DINNERTIME

Normally a solitary animal, the devil regularly shares meals with others, and it's a very noisy eater, using 11 different vocal sounds to communicate as it feeds. The ultimate eating machine, it mostly scavenges carrion (dead and diseased animals such as dying sheep and roadkill), which helps clean up the environment and prevent the spread of disease. It will even dig up animal corpses. With the strongest bite (for its size) of any land animal on earth, the devil can bite through metal traps. Its jaw can open up to 80 degrees, and it is capable of eating every part of an animal, including bones and fur. When eating large animals, the devil will rip open the belly and eat the digestive tract, sometimes sitting inside the cavity while eating. Although it prefers larger animals like wombats, it does hunt small mammals like bettongs and potoroos. It will also eat birds, fish, insects, tadpoles, frogs, reptiles and fruit.

80°

LITTLE DEVILS

Males fight for a female, and she will mate with the dominant one. He then guards her to prevent other males muscling in. Females give birth (while standing up!) to as many as 30 young. Babies are called pups, joeys or imps (little devils!). They are pink, hairless and tiny at birth, about the size of a grain of rice. As females have just four teats, the race is on to get to the backwards-facing pouch, and only four pups survive. Sometimes, the young can be seen riding on their mother's back as she hunts.

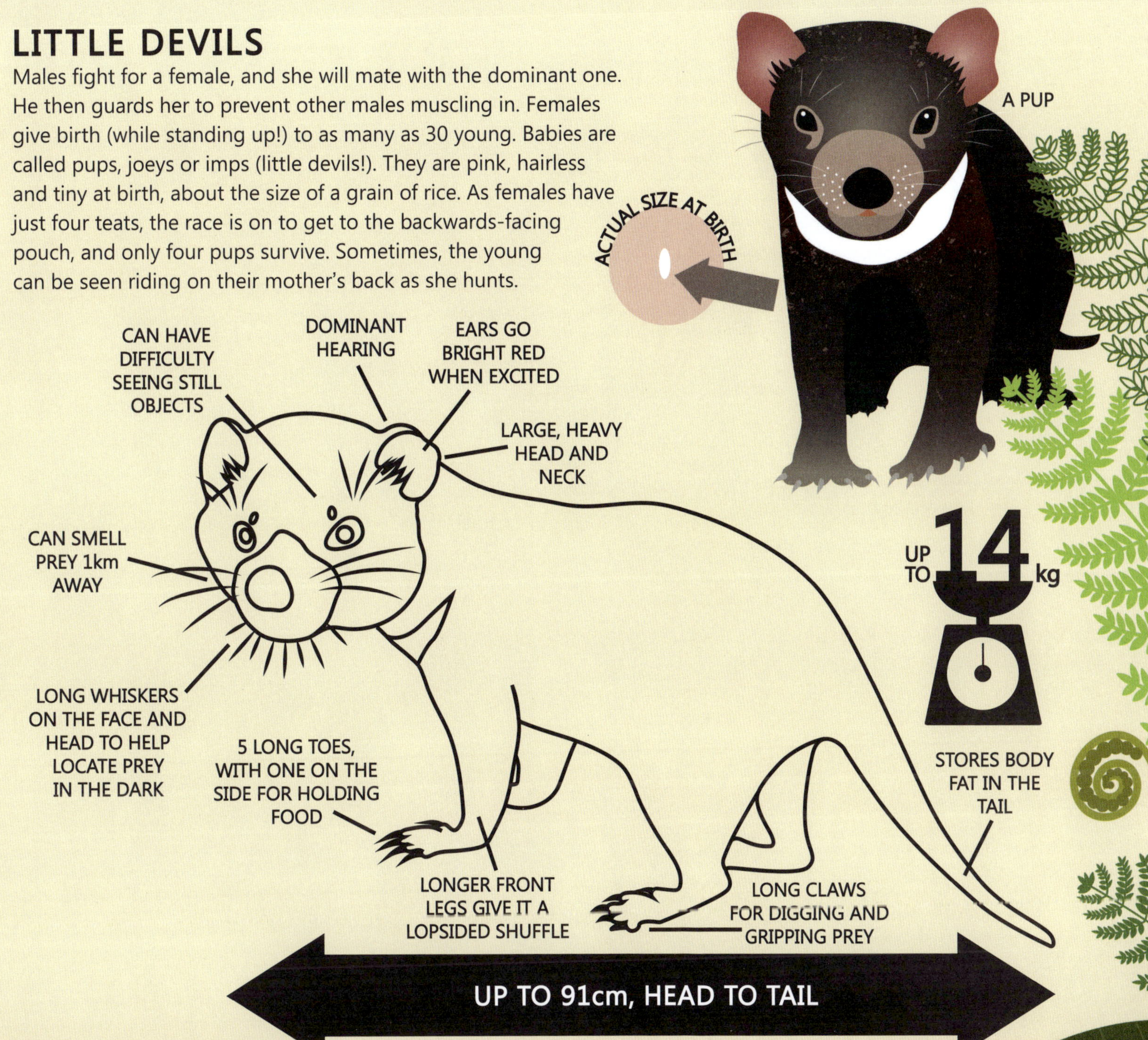

FLIGHT OR FIGHT

This ferocious creature has a pungent odour when stressed, and if threatened, it will yawn at its foe. It ambles along slowly but can gallop quickly if need be, loping along with its hind feet together. It can swim well, and younger devils can climb trees.

COMMUNAL LOO

When home ranges overlap, devils create their own communal toilet, returning there to poop. It's called a devil latrine and is used as a kind of notice board, leaving 'messages' for others about their activity.

TUMOURS

Since the late 1990s, devil facial tumour disease has killed over 80 per cent of the population (in diseased areas), and the species overall is now endangered. This disease is contagious, and quickly passes from one devil to another. The conservation project on Maria Island is disease-free.

EN

THE FLYING FOX

(*Pteropus*)

FLIGHTY MAMMALS

A whopping one-quarter of all mammal species on earth are bats. In Australia, there are over 90 species and two types—mega and micro. Megabats are larger and feed on fruit, nectar and pollen. Flying foxes belong to this group. Also known as fruit bats, the four mainland species of flying fox are spectacled, black, grey-headed and little red. Fossil teeth found in Queensland date the flying fox back 55 million years.

HEY, GOOD LOOKING

During the day, flying foxes roost together in treetops, and sleep hanging by one foot, with wings wrapped around the body. They spend many hours each day grooming, licking their wings, chattering and fanning themselves. They flap their wings to cool down, and wash by peeing on themselves!

GADDING ABOUT

Flying foxes can fly at up to 40km/h, and can use wind drafts, too. Bats are the only mammal capable of powered flight.

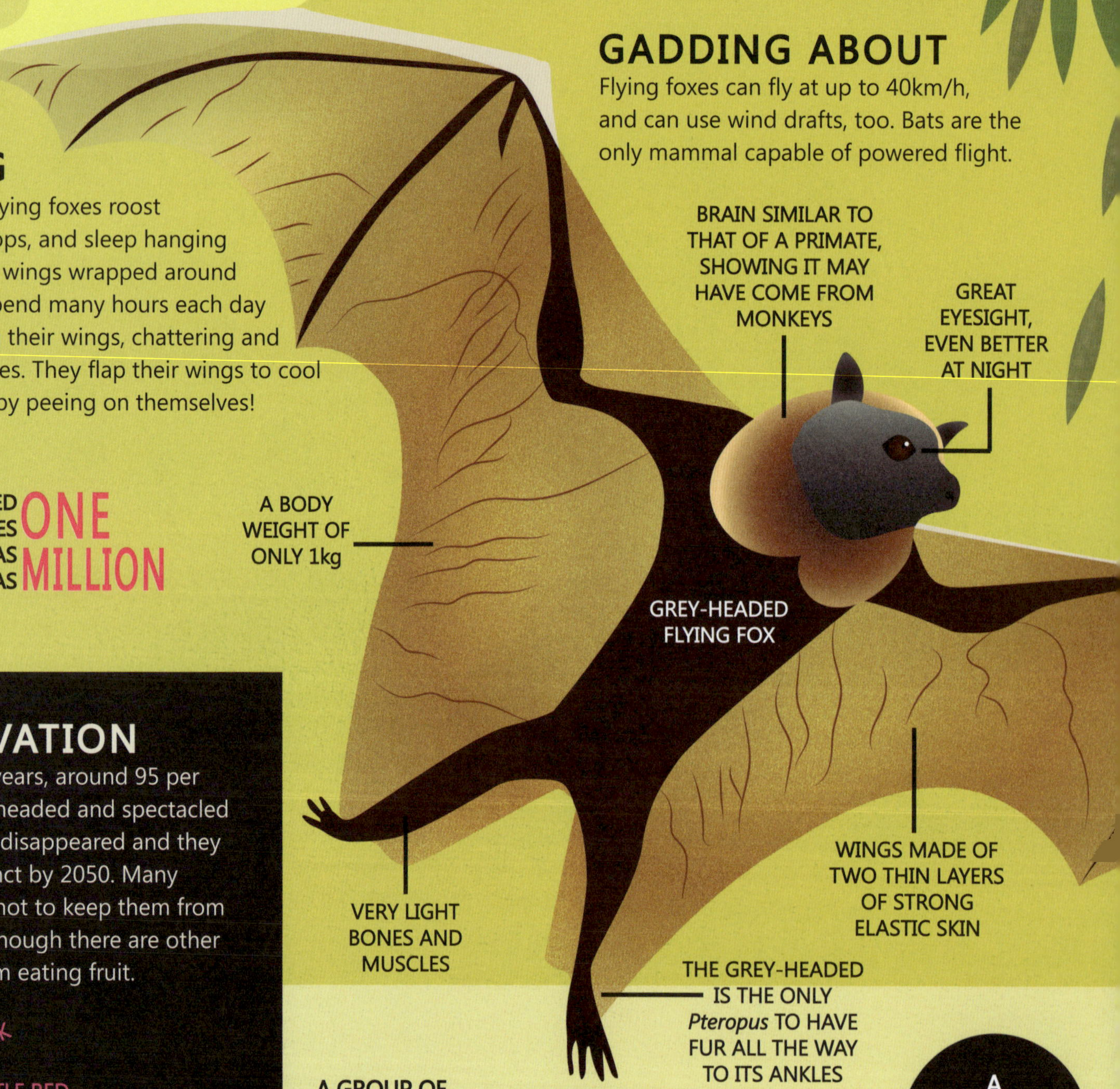

BRAIN SIMILAR TO THAT OF A PRIMATE, SHOWING IT MAY HAVE COME FROM MONKEYS

GREAT EYESIGHT, EVEN BETTER AT NIGHT

THE LITTLE RED LIVES IN COLONIES NUMBERING AS MANY AS ONE MILLION

A BODY WEIGHT OF ONLY 1kg

GREY-HEADED FLYING FOX

VERY LIGHT BONES AND MUSCLES

WINGS MADE OF TWO THIN LAYERS OF STRONG ELASTIC SKIN

THE GREY-HEADED IS THE ONLY *Pteropus* TO HAVE FUR ALL THE WAY TO ITS ANKLES

A GROUP OF FLYING FOXES IS CALLED A COLONY

A WINGSPAN OF UP TO 1m

CONSERVATION

Over the last 30 years, around 95 per cent of the grey-headed and spectacled flying foxes have disappeared and they may be fully extinct by 2050. Many flying foxes are shot to keep them from fruit trees, even though there are other ways to stop them eating fruit.

LC: BLACK, LITTLE RED

VU: SPECTACLED, GREY-HEADED

GREY-HEADED
(*Pteropus poliocephalus*)
Dark grey fur, red collar and light grey head. The largest bat in Australia and one of the biggest in the world, with a body length of up to 29cm.

BLACK
(*Pteropus alecto*)
Short black fur with reddish brown mantle. Weighs up to 710g. It also lives in parts of Papua New Guinea and Indonesia. There are four subspecies.

SPECTACLED
(*Pteropus conspicillatus*)
Brown fur with light yellow on shoulders, neck, back and face. Body length up to 25cm. Lives in far north Queensland, and in Papua New Guinea and adjoining islands.

LITTLE RED
(*Pteropus scapulatus*)
Brownish red fur with a red collar. It is the smallest flying fox on mainland Australia. It has the largest range of all species.

CHOW TIME

Flying foxes feed at night, and many of their favourite plants have white flowers, making them easier to see. They love the fruit, flowers, nectar and pollen of native trees, and pollen is a major source of protein. Surviving on a mostly liquid diet, they chew leaves and fruit to extract the juice and seeds. Flying foxes are an important part of the ecosystem, as they are able to spread pollen and seeds over hundreds of kilometres. They use their excellent sense of smell to locate nectar and ripe fruit, and thanks to great night vision, they don't need to echo-locate (use sound to find food or to navigate). To drink, they lick the dew from leaves or swoop over waterways and then lick the water from their belly fur.

BATS IN THE BELFRY

Flying foxes are social animals. They chirp and squabble and use mating and warning calls. They live in groups, and come together in even larger groups to mate. Males have a scent gland on their shoulders that is rubbed onto branches to mark territory. One male guards several females and young in a 'harem'.

LITTLE ONES

Flying foxes give birth to just one baby, which is born furry, with open eyes. The baby suckles on one of two teats located under Mum's wings, holding onto the teat with two milk teeth. During the day, the female shields her baby with her wings. At night, she soars through the air in search of food, with her baby on her back. When they're bigger, babies are left in 'day care' with other flying foxes, and are able to fly on their own at just 3 months old.

HOME

spectacled

MARSUPIALS

A POUCHFUL OF CUTE

Marsupials have inhabited Australia for over 50 million years. Thought to have originated in South America, they migrated to Australia when both countries were connected (as part of Gondwana). When Australia broke off from Antarctica and moved north, the evolution of unique Australian marsupials began, and they are now the second-oldest type of mammal found in Australia (second to the monotremes). The name marsupial comes from the Latin 'marsupium', which means pouch. Marsupial babies grow inside a membranous egg inside the mother's belly. Undeveloped at birth, they must crawl their way to the pouch, where they'll suckle milk and grow. Most Australian marsupials are nocturnal. They live in all kinds of habitats—forests, riverlands, deserts—though most avoid colder climates. There are no truly flying or aquatic marsupials, and all use two or four legs to move around.

TREE-KANGAROOS

(*Dendrolagus*) There are two species of tree-kangaroo in Australia—Lumholtz's tree-kangaroo and Bennett's tree-kangaroo. Living in the rainforests of far north Queensland, they are the only true arboreal macropods, meaning the only tree-dweller of the kangaroo family. They have short, broad hind feet with curved nails and a sponge-like grip on the soles. They are slow and clumsy on the ground but agile in the treetops, where their tails help them balance. Tree-kangaroos hug trees with their forearms and use their back legs to hop up the trunk. They can leap up to 9 metres and can jump to the ground from twice that height, without being hurt. They give birth to just one joey each year, and their main diet is leaves and fruit.

GREATER BILBY

(*Macrotis lagotis*) Greater bilbies live in arid areas of central Australia and are now considered vulnerable. They make a complicated system of burrows (up to a dozen) that spiral down so predators can't get in. They have a long tail and big rabbit-like ears, making them our official native Easter Bunny. These large ears help keep them cool. Their eyesight is poor, but they have excellent hearing and smell. Greater bilbies are nocturnal omnivores and don't need to drink water. They dig for food and retrieve it with their very long tongues. A mother will be pregnant for just 2 weeks before giving birth. Sadly, the lesser bilby is thought to have been extinct since the 1950s or 1960s.

QUOKKA

(Setonix brachyurus)

Resembling very small kangaroos, the majority of quokkas live on Rottnest Island, off the coast of Perth. One of the first Australian mammals to be seen by Europeans, they were mistaken by the Dutch for giant rats. In fact, the island was named 'Rottenest', which comes from the Dutch word 'rattennest' meaning 'rat nest'. Quokkas have little fear of humans and seem to love having 'selfies' taken with tourists. Don't touch them, though. It's illegal, and they could get very sick. Better to take a picture and let these adorable creatures be.

GILBERT'S POTOROO

(Potorous gilbertii)

Officially the world's rarest marsupial, it was thought extinct for 120 years. In 1994, 40 were found near Albany in Western Australia. The potoroo is still critically endangered, and a captive breeding facility has been set up to keep it away from predators.

NUMBAT

(Myrmecobius fasciatus)

The numbat is the only existing member of its family, the Myrmecobiidae. It has no close relation, though some say it could have been related to the extinct thylacine (Tasmanian tiger). Unlike most other marsupials, the numbat is active during the day (diurnal) and sleeps at night. While it has a mouthful of small teeth, it rarely chews. It has a long, narrow tongue coated with sticky saliva, and will slurp up 20,000 termites a day.

EN

SADLY, MANY AUSTRALIAN MARSUPIALS ARE THREATENED OR ENDANGERED

COMMON OR BARE-NOSED
(Vombatus ursinus)
UP TO 50kg

NORTHERN HAIRY-NOSED
(Lasiorhinus krefftii)
UP TO 40kg

SOUTHERN HAIRY-NOSED
(Lasiorhinus latifrons)
UP TO 38kg

WOMBATS

(Vombatidae) The second-largest marsupial in Australia (after kangaroos), and one of our most beloved animals, the wombat is a true digging machine. It eats plants and gets most of its water from them, too. In fact, a wombat can live for months without a single drink! Due to a very slow metabolism, it takes about 2 weeks for a wombat to digest a meal. Although it has very short legs, it can run at up to 40km/h. Wombat burrows can be up to 20 metres long and 3.5 metres deep. If a predator enters, the wombat may crush it against the burrow wall. To mark their territory, wombats leave small piles of dung, released in small cubes to stop them rolling away. There are three living species of wombat—the common or bare-nosed, the southern hairy-nosed and the northern hairy-nosed. Genetically, the two hairy-nosed wombats are very different to the common wombat. Scientists believe there are an astonishing 4 to 5 million years separating them on the family tree!

THE DUGONG

(*Dugong dugon*)

THE COW OF THE SEA

With the body of a seal, the tail of a dolphin, an elephant's tusks, enormous lungs and the grazing habits of a cow, the dugong is the only strictly herbivorous marine mammal. Early sailors mistook dugongs for mermaids, thanks to their long bodies and large teats (located under the female's paddle-like fins). Also called sea cows, sea pigs and sea camels, they are more closely related to elephants than to any marine mammal. One of the four living species of the order Sirenia, dugongs are thought to have evolved from four-legged land animals. Fossil records date back 60 million years.

CRUISING

The dugong swims by moving its tail up and down like a whale, turning and slowing with its flippers. It usually swims at around 10km/h, with a top speed of more than 25km/h. It can even 'walk' on its fins on the sea floor, and can stand on its tail with its head above the water's surface.

THE HUNTED

Prized for meat, skin, bones and oil, the dugong has been hunted for thousands of years. For Indigenous people, the dugong is a valuable source of protein. They also use it in ceremonies and for community and cultural purposes.

DIVES UP TO
12
TIMES AN HOUR

OUT TO PASTURE

The dugong grazes on seagrass meadows, and will dive as deep as 30 metres in search of seagrass. Using its hoover-like mouth, it rips up seagrass, roots and all. Feeding is a messy affair. The dugong shakes its head to get rid of all the sand, then grinds the grass on horny mouth pads. It can eat up to 50 kilograms of seagrass in one day, and its long intestine (25 metres) helps digest the plant fibres.

THICK SKIN

NO DORSAL FIN

EAR HOLES

SMALL, INEFFECTIVE EYES

TWO SMALL TUSKS HIDDEN UNDER THE SKIN

NOSTRILS CLOSE WHILE UNDER WATER

DOWNTURNED SNOUT

LARGE MOUTH WITH MUSCULAR UPPER LIP

PADDLE-LIKE FLIPPERS

THE DUGONG CRUISES AT AROUND 10m BELOW THE SURFACE

SEAGRASS ALL DAY MENU

Halophila ovalis

Halodule pinifolia

Amphibolis griffithii

Halophila spinulosa

Thalassia hemprichii

HELLO, BABY!

Males use their tusks to fight each other for a female, who will give birth to one baby every 3 to 7 years. The birth occurs in shallow waters, and as soon as a calf is born, the mother pushes it to the surface to take a breath. The baby will suckle for 18 months. Mothers and calves have a strong bond, and the baby will stay with Mum until maturity.

BODY IMAGE

Measuring up to 3.3 metres long, the dugong's body is covered in tiny bristles, especially around the mouth, which help it sense its surroundings. With poor eyesight, it relies on well-developed hearing and an acute sense of smell. To help it stay submerged, the dugong's ribs and other large bones are heavy and solid, with little or no marrow. Its bones are some of the most dense in the animal kingdom.

STAYS UNDER WATER AROUND 2.7 MINUTES

UP TO 570 kg

LONG KIDNEYS COPE WITH A SALTY HABITAT

TAPERED BODY

NO HIND LIMBS

FLUKED TAIL

GOOD VIBRATIONS

The dugong communicates like a dolphin, with chirps, whistles, barks and other echoing sounds. Although they are communal creatures, they generally live in pairs.

A GROUP OF DUGONGS IS CALLED A HERD

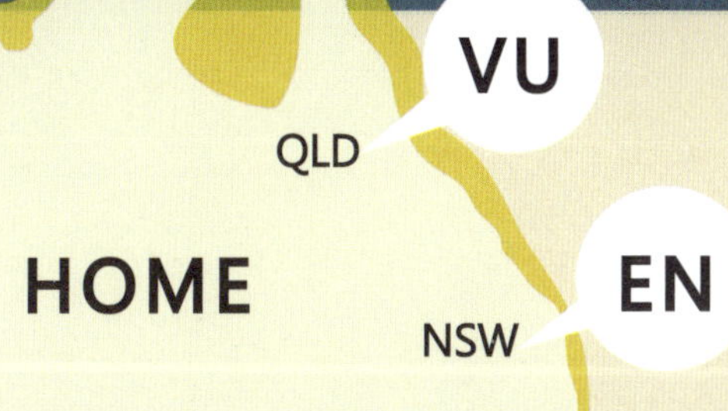

HOME

Found in warm coastal waters from the western Pacific Ocean to the east coast of Africa, the largest dugong concentration is found from Shark Bay in Western Australia to Moreton Bay in Queensland, with a small population drifting along the coast of New South Wales. Dugongs prefer shallow, protected areas such as bays, mangrove channels and inter-reefal waters. They can travel more than 10 kilometres offshore.

THE THORNY DEVIL

(*Moloch horridus*)

LC

DEVIL, DRAGON, LIZARD, TOAD?

Also known as the thorny dragon, mountain devil, thorny lizard, devil lizard, horned lizard and thorny toad, this fierce-looking creature may have a rhino-like head, but it's actually a small, gentle reptile. Found in the arid scrublands and deserts that cover most of central Australia, this comical lizard walks like a wind-up toy—rocking, hovering, freezing, stopping and starting. Thorny devils lead a mostly solitary life, only coming together to mate.

THE REPTILIAN CAMEL

The thorny devil doesn't drink water the 'regular' way. With moisture so scarce in the desert, this spiky creature walks through dewy grass, collecting droplets on its ridged skin. By opening and closing its mouth, the water is worked along the lizard's textured body to its mouth. Incredibly, devils sometimes bury themselves in wet sand and trap tiny beads of moisture against the skin in this way, too!

A THORNY DEVIL CAN LIVE UP TO **20** YEARS

HOME SWEET HOME

The thorny devil lives in a shallow burrow. It doesn't like extreme heat or cold, and at night will bury itself in sand to keep warm. It also digs down into the sand to protect itself from burning desert temperatures. To keep hydrated, it can excrete excess salt from its body.

A GROUP OF THORNY DEVILS IS CALLED A **LOUNGE**

BABY DEVILS

The males attract females with elaborate courtship rituals, including head-bobbing and leg-waving. The females give off a scent that attracts males, but after mating, he's not very loyal. He leaves immediately to look for more females. The female lays eggs in an underground nesting burrow, losing 40 per cent of her body weight in the process. She covers the eggs with sand, and when the babies hatch, they eat their eggshells before digging their way out of the nest. By then, Mum is long gone!

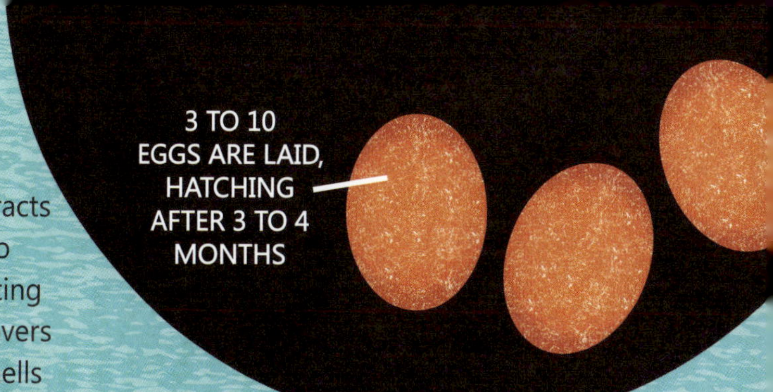

3 TO 10 EGGS ARE LAID, HATCHING AFTER 3 TO 4 MONTHS

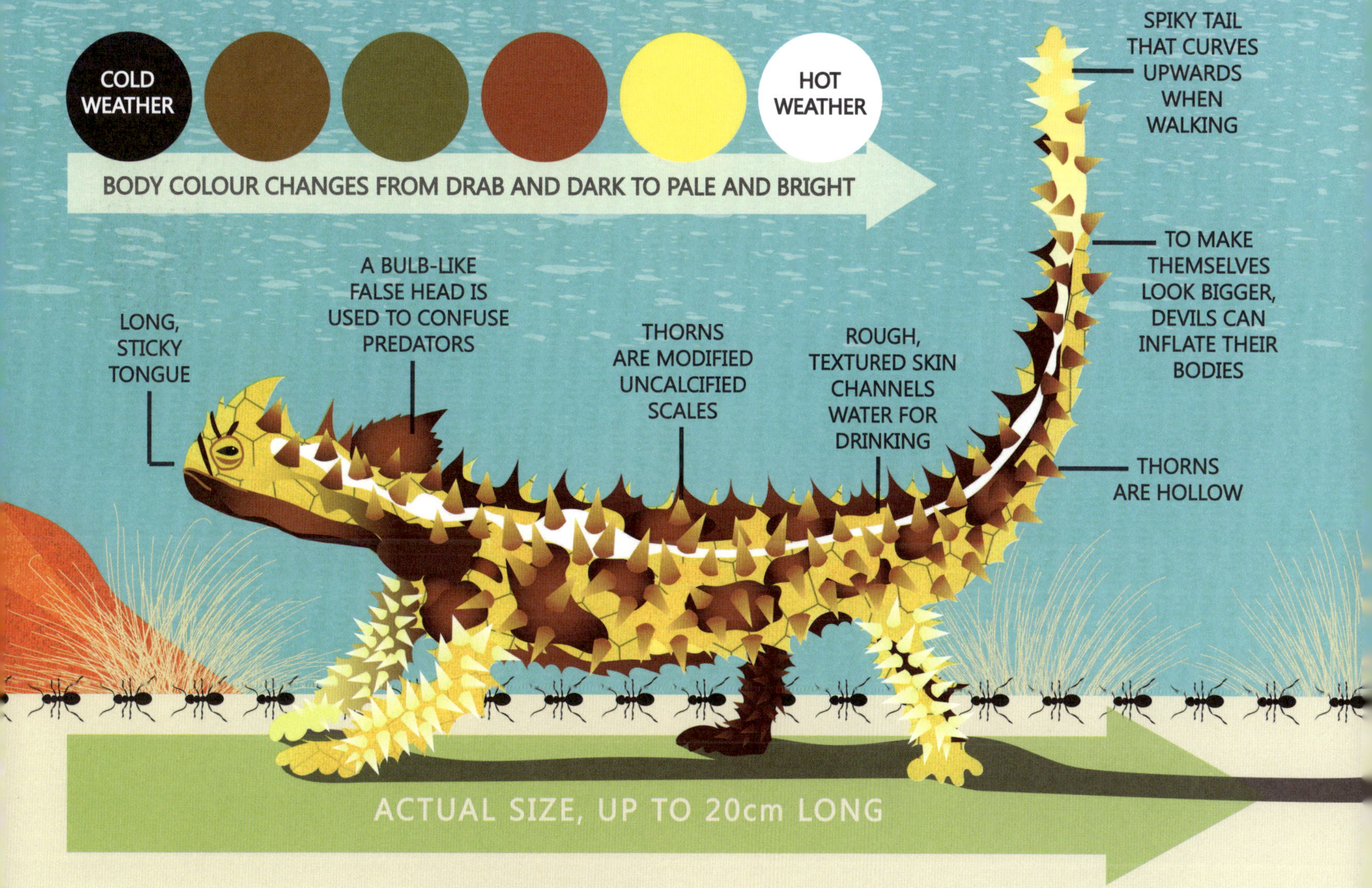

COLD WEATHER

HOT WEATHER

BODY COLOUR CHANGES FROM DRAB AND DARK TO PALE AND BRIGHT

LONG, STICKY TONGUE

A BULB-LIKE FALSE HEAD IS USED TO CONFUSE PREDATORS

THORNS ARE MODIFIED UNCALCIFIED SCALES

ROUGH, TEXTURED SKIN CHANNELS WATER FOR DRINKING

SPIKY TAIL THAT CURVES UPWARDS WHEN WALKING

TO MAKE THEMSELVES LOOK BIGGER, DEVILS CAN INFLATE THEIR BODIES

THORNS ARE HOLLOW

ACTUAL SIZE, UP TO 20cm LONG

CHOW TIME

Most of the thorny devil's diet is made up of black ants. It can eat as many as 2,500 in one sitting. When it locates a trail of ants, it either uses its sticky tongue to lick them up one by one, or just opens its mouth to let the ants walk in!

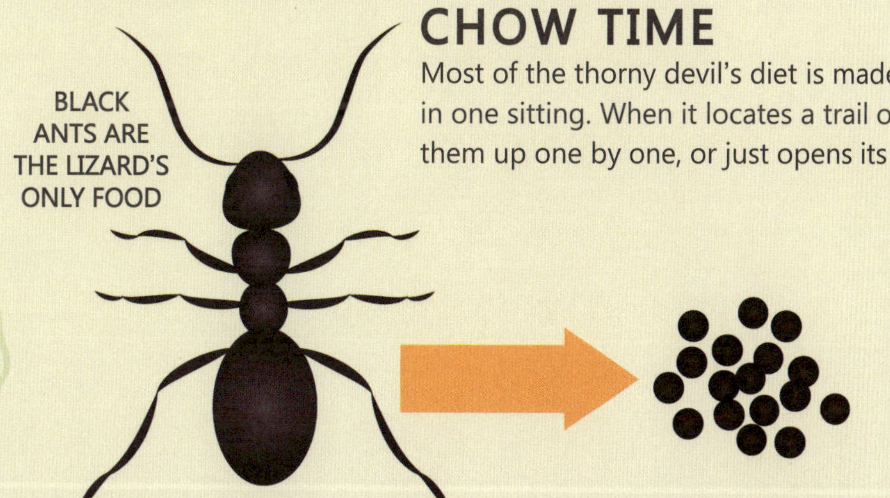

SKELETON POOP

Devils have distinctive poop. Droppings are glossy, black spheroids that crumble easily to reveal the exoskeletons of ants. These lizards have a specific place to poop, well away from where they feed and bask in the sun.

EXTINCTION

IT'S NOT GOOD NEWS

We are now in the Holocene epoch (from 10,000 years ago until today). Changes to our environment and fauna have occurred since Indigenous people arrived in Australia tens of thousands of years ago, but the greatest and most damaging changes have occurred in the last 200 years, since Europeans arrived. Australia now has the worst mammal extinction rate in the world. As our country further develops and climate change takes hold, our most unique, most curious creatures are at greatest risk.

CR

LORD HOWE ISLAND STICK INSECT

CRITICALLY ENDANGERED

- FRESHWATER SNAIL (*Beddomeia tumida*)
- LORD HOWE ISLAND STICK INSECT (*Dryococelus australis*)
- GREY NURSE SHARK (*Carcharias taurus*) – east coast population
- BORNEMISSZA'S STAG BEETLE (*Hoplogonus bornemisszai*)
- LEADBEATER'S POSSUM (*Gymnobelideus leadbeateri*)
- WESTERN SWAMP TORTOISE (*Pseudemydura umbrina*)
- SOUTHERN CORROBOREE FROG (*Pseudophryne corroboree*)
- ORANGE-BELLIED PARROT (*Neophema chrysogaster*)
- DERWENT RIVER SEA STAR (*Marginaster littoralis*)
- GILBERT'S POTOROO (*Potorous gilbertii*)
- ARMOURED MISTFROG (*Litoria lorica*)
- WOYLIE (*Bettongia penicillata ogilbyi*)
- HERALD PETREL (*Pterodroma heraldica*)
- FRESHWATER SAWFISH (*Pristis pristis*)
- MARGARET RIVER BURROWING CRAYFISH (*Engaewa pseudoreducta*)
- MARGARET RIVER HAIRY MARRON (*Cherax tenuimanus*)
- SOUTHERN BENT-WING BAT (*Miniopterus orianae bassanii*)
- SHORT-NOSED SEA SNAKE (*Aipysurus apraefrontalis*)
- MOUNTAIN PYGMY-POSSUM (*Burramys parvus*)
- RED-FINNED BLUE-EYE FISH (*Scaturiginichthys vermeilipinnis*)
- NORTHERN HAIRY-NOSED WOMBAT (*Lasiorhinus krefftii*)

GILBERT'S POTOROO

CR

THERE ARE MANY ENDANGERED SPECIES, BUT THESE ANIMALS ARE ON THE BRINK OF EXTINCTION. SOME COULD BE GONE WITHIN JUST A FEW YEARS.

NORTHERN HAIRY-NOSED WOMBAT

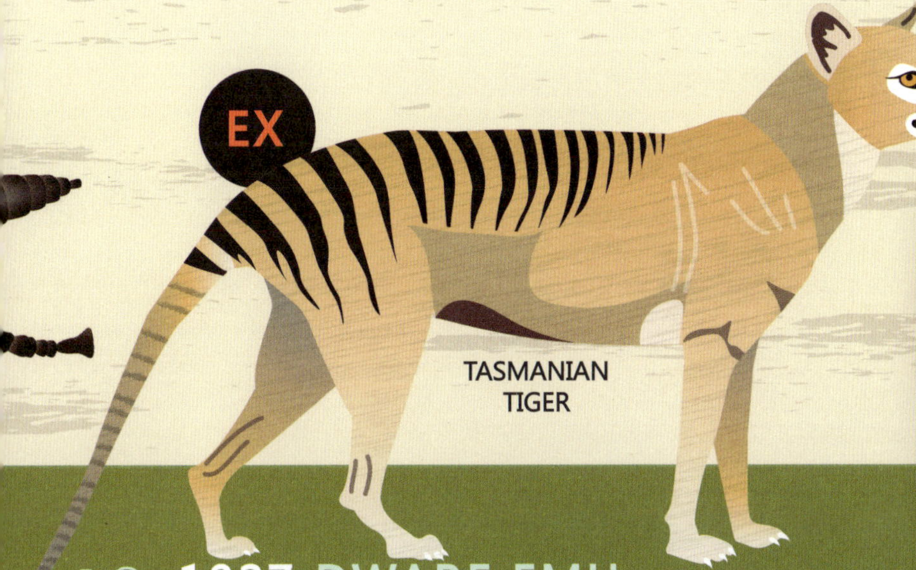

EX – EXTINCT
EW – EXTINCT IN THE WILD
CR – CRITICALLY ENDANGERED
EN – ENDANGERED
VU – VULNERABLE
NT – NEAR THREATENED
LC – LEAST CONCERN

RECENT EXTINCTIONS

1827 DWARF EMU *(Dromaius baudinianus)*

1857 WHITE-FOOTED RABBIT-RAT *(Conilurus albipes)*

1896 SHORT-TAILED HOPPING MOUSE *(Notomys amplus)*

1927 PARADISE PARROT *(Psephotus pulcherrimus)*

This exceptionally colourful parrot lived in pairs or small groups, making nests in hollowed-out termite mounds. Their tails were very long, despite spending most of their time on the ground. The bird was last seen in 1927.

1928 LORD HOWE GERYGONE *(Gerygone insularis)*

1936 TASMANIAN TIGER *(Thylacinus cynocephalus)*

Probably our most famous extinct species, the Tasmanian tiger was the largest known carnivorous marsupial of modern times. This nocturnal, shy animal was the last member of its family, Thylacinidae. Extensive hunting was blamed for its extinction, and the last known tiger died in captivity at Hobart Zoo in 1936. There have been hundreds of unconfirmed sightings of the tiger in the wild since then, most recently in Victoria in 2008.

1950s PIG-FOOTED BANDICOOT *(Chaeropus ecaudatus)*

1960s LESSER BILBY *(Macrotis leucura)*

Around the size of a rabbit, the lesser bilby lived in the deserts of Central Australia. It was nocturnal, omnivorous and quite aggressive. The oral tradition of local Indigenous people suggests it may have become extinct in the 1960s. Its less aggressive cousin, the greater bilby, is now considered vulnerable.

1972 LAKE PEDDER EARTHWORM *(Hypolimnus pedderensis)*

1980s SOUTHERN GASTRIC-BROODING FROG *(Rheobatrachus silus)*

This Queensland frog was unique in that it incubated its young. The female would swallow her own eggs, then would stop feeding, allowing the babies to develop in her stomach. When ready to 'hatch', she would open her throat and the babies would crawl out of her mouth. Both the southern and northern gastric-brooding frogs became extinct in the mid-1980s. A cloning attempt known as the Lazarus Project began in an attempt to resurrect the species, and in 2013 there was a major breakthrough when embryos were successfully cloned. Further work is needed to keep embryos alive.

EXTINCTION

MEGAFAUNA MONSTERS

Megafauna were giant, more ferocious versions of some of our modern-day native animals. These giant creatures, including echidnas, platypus, koalas and kangaroos, roamed our land during the Pleistocene era (or the last Ice Age), when Indigenous people first arrived in Australia. Scientists believe hunting and fire management may have contributed to the extinction of the megafauna, which died out 46,000 years ago.

GIANT ECHIDNA (*Zaglossus hacketti*) Long-beaked and around a metre high, the giant echnidna is the largest monotreme that ever lived. Its sticky tongue is said to have been 54 centimetres long. The average human tongue is just 7cm long.

GIANT PLATYPUS (*Obdurodon tharalkooschild*) Nicknamed 'Godzilla', this mega platypus was a metre in length, or around twice the size of the modern version. It also had a full set of teeth. Although it is born with teeth, the modern platypus loses them by adulthood.

GIANT KANGAROO (*Procoptodon goliah*) The largest known roo that ever lived, this giant stood up to 2.7 metres tall and could weigh a whopping 240 kilograms. Each foot had a single toe that resembled a horse's hoof, and the front paws had large claws that were probably used for pulling on branches to reach leaves. Like modern-day kangaroos, it was a herbivore.

GIANT KOALA (*Phascolarctos stirtoni*) Although only a third larger than the modern koala, this 'giant' is thought to be the largest tree-dwelling marsupial ever. The modern-day koala is a relative of the giant koala, but, amazingly, it's not a direct descendent.

GIANT WOMBAT (*Phascolonus*) Weighing up to 200 kilograms, this giant wombat lived alongside its distant relative, the Diprotodon. A two-million-year-old fossil of this wombat was found near a Quinkana crocodile at Tea Tree Cave in Queensland.

STIRTON'S THUNDER BIRD (*Dromornis stirtoni*) Nicknamed the Demon Duck of Doom, this prehistoric flightless bird is said to have been the tallest and heaviest bird that ever lived—up to 3 metres tall and 650 kilograms in weight. It had a long neck, stubby wings and strong legs. Despite having a powerful beak, it's thought to have been a herbivore.

MARSUPIAL LION (*Thylacoleo carnifex*) At up to 160 kilograms and 150 centimetres from head to tail, the marsupial lion was the biggest Australian carnivorous mammal ever known. It had special shearing teeth and large, semi-opposable thumb claws, good for tearing prey apart. Its hindfeet had a roughened pad, making it capable of climbing trees to drop down on its prey. It was found throughout Australia.

QUINKANA CROCODILE (*Quinkana fortirostrum*) This mega croc was one of the top predators of early Australia, with long legs and serrated teeth. It reached an astonishing 6 metres in length.

DIPROTODON (*Diprotodon optatum*) The largest known marsupial, the Diprotodon resembled a giant wombat—the size of a rhino. The largest fossil specimen measured 3 metres long and 2 metres high at the shoulder, and weighed almost 3 tonnes. The closest surviving relatives of the Diprotodon are wombats and koalas.

BLUFF DOWNS GIANT PYTHON (*Liasis dubudingala*) This Queensland snake lived during the early Pliocene era and is believed to have grown up to 10 metres long. This would make it over 2 metres longer than the modern world's longest snake, the Asiatic reticulated python.

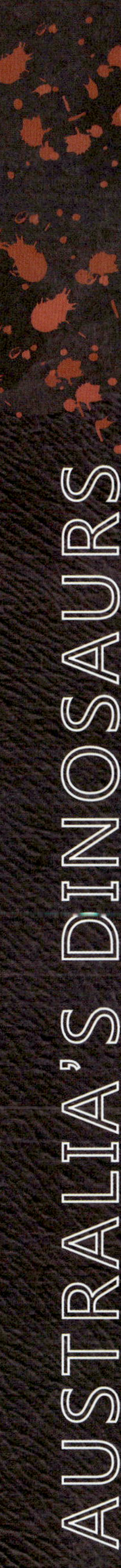

Dinosaurs lived during the Mesozoic era, roughly 230 million to 65 million years ago, when they suddenly and rapidly died out. The Mesozoic was divided into three periods: the Triassic, Jurassic and Cretaceous. The Triassic was when all land on earth was connected in one big mass called Pangaea. During the Jurassic period, Pangaea split in two, forming Laurasia in the north and Gondwana in the south. In the Cretaceous period, land began forming into the continents we know today. It was also when flowering plants and insects (including bees) appeared . . . and when the sudden extinction of dinosaurs occurred. This extinction allowed for the rapid development of modern-day mammals and birds.

The dinosaurs of Australia are not well known, with only around 17 well-defined species, and many fragmented pieces that are still being put together. These four ferocious creatures are among the better known Aussie versions, and more are being pieced together (literally!) by the day.

MYTHUNGA PTERODACTYL (*Mythunga camara*) Mythunga was a flying reptile with a box-like snout and large, interlocking teeth. With an enormous span of 4.7 metres, its wings were similar to bats—skin membranes supported by elongated fourth fingers. It lived near the Eromanga Sea, a vast inland lake of cool water covering central Australia.

KRONOSAURUS (*Kronosaurus queenslandicus*) A short-necked pliosaur, kronosaurus fossils found in Queensland suggest it weighed as much as 9 tonnes and measured from 10 to 12 metres long, making it one of the largest marine reptiles ever. Its teeth were the size and shape of small bananas. With four flippers and a short tail, it lived in the Eromanga Sea and was a fast swimmer.

AUSTRALIAN ICHTHYOSAUR (*Platypterygius longmani*) At up to 7 metres long, this dolphin-like marine reptile roamed the Eromanga Sea during the early Cretaceous period. It was an apex predator, feeding on fish and cephalopods, and had large eyes that helped it spot prey in dark waters.

LIGHTNING CLAW (*Megaraptor*) Nicknamed 'Lightning Claw', this megaraptorid was discovered in the 1990s in opal fields southwest of Lightning Ridge in New South Wales. Dating back 110 million years, the megaraptorid family may have evolved in Australia then branched out across Gondwana. It would have been about 7 metres in length, which would make it our biggest carnivorous dinosaur (currently known).

THE ANIMAL FAMILY TREE

Life on earth is a miraculous thing, and living beings have been evolving for millennia. The animal kingdom is incredibly rich and varied, and scientists are still coming up with ways to classify animals into 'families' that help us better understand these amazing creatures. Over countless generations, animals have evolved to fit their environments, and the most adaptable animals are the ones that have survived. The different climates, environments and challenges of living on planet Earth have led to the appearance of the many curious animals included in this book. There are almost countless species and variations of species. Below, you will find links between some of our more well-known animals.

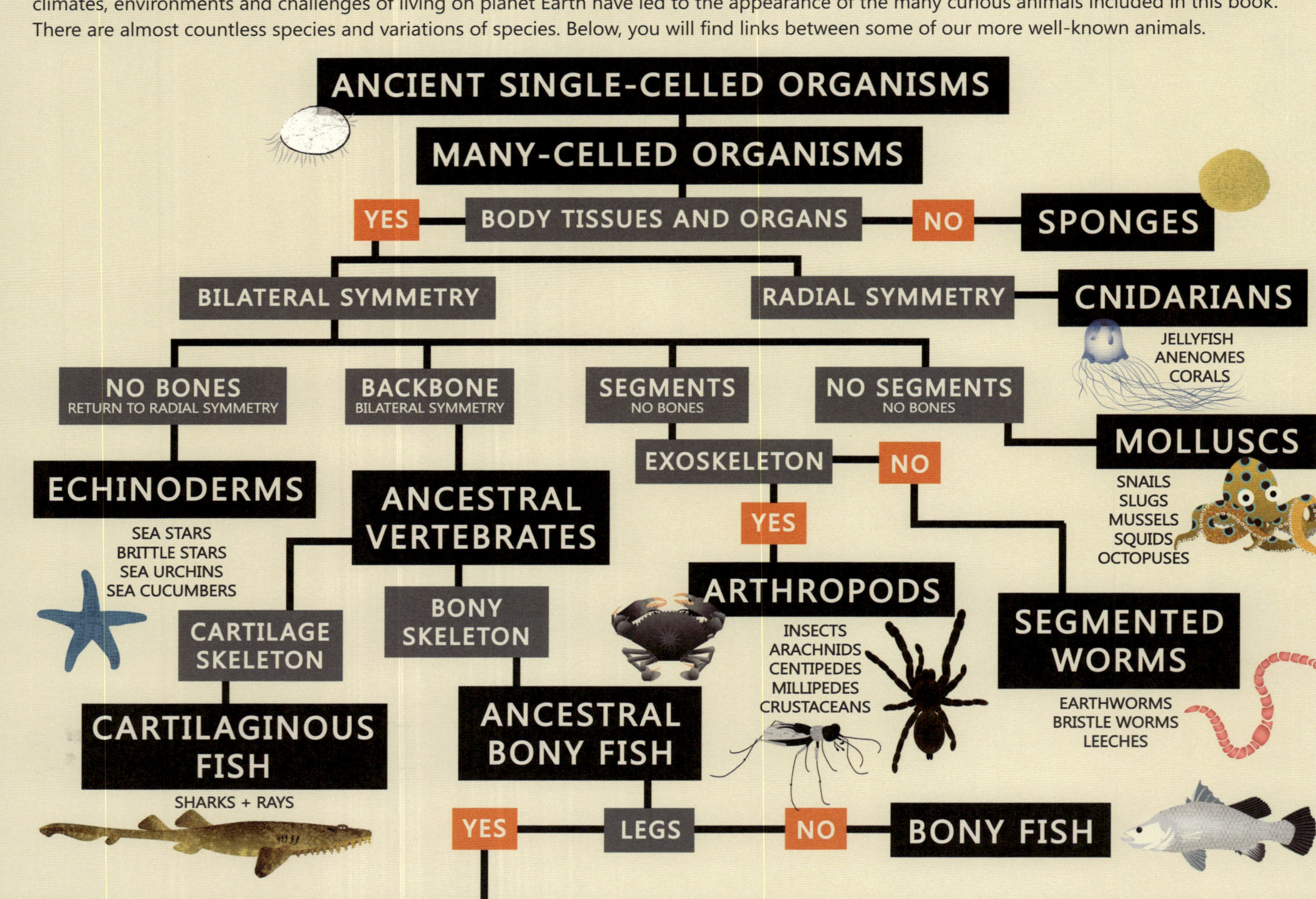

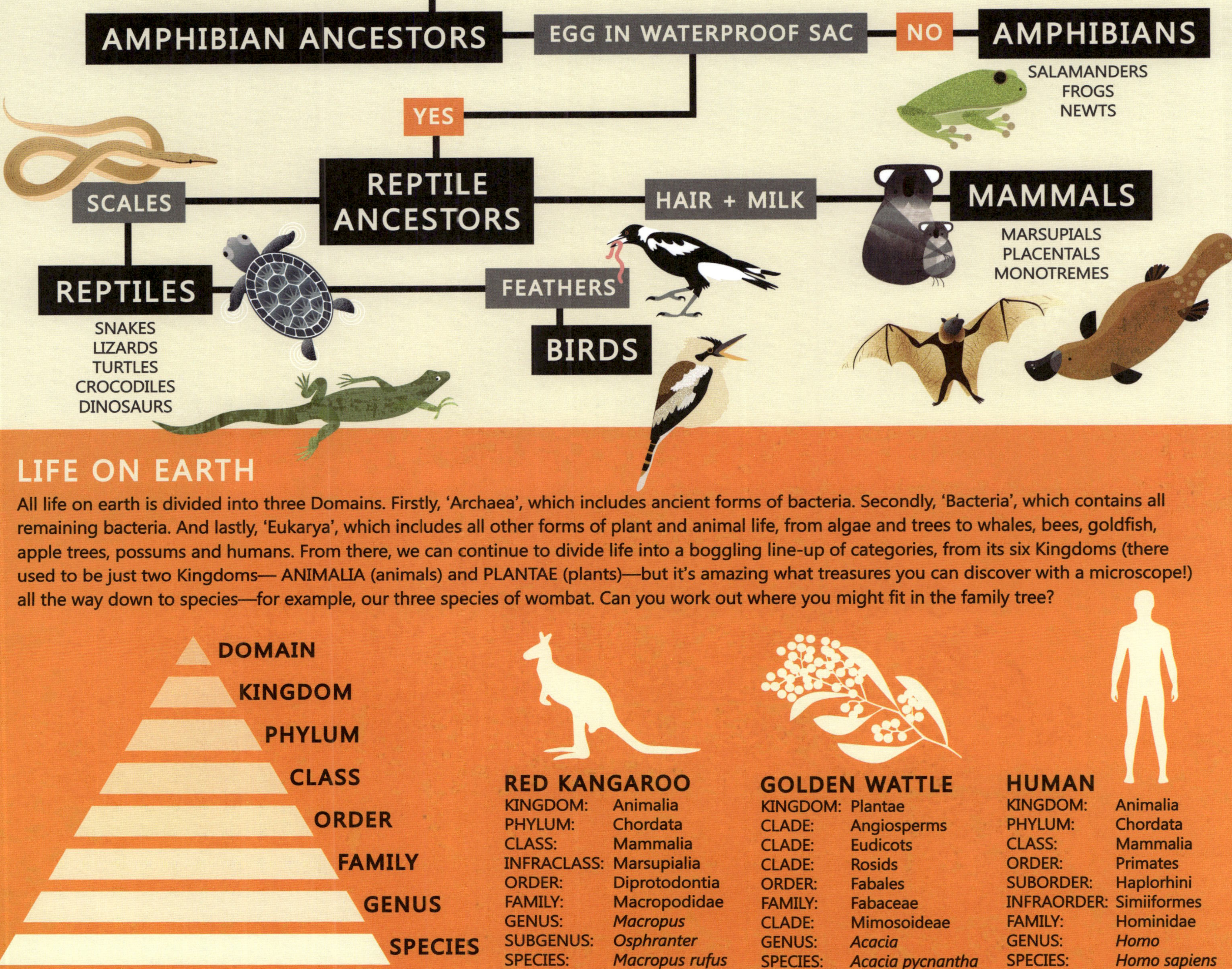

LIFE ON EARTH

All life on earth is divided into three Domains. Firstly, 'Archaea', which includes ancient forms of bacteria. Secondly, 'Bacteria', which contains all remaining bacteria. And lastly, 'Eukarya', which includes all other forms of plant and animal life, from algae and trees to whales, bees, goldfish, apple trees, possums and humans. From there, we can continue to divide life into a boggling line-up of categories, from its six Kingdoms (there used to be just two Kingdoms— ANIMALIA (animals) and PLANTAE (plants)—but it's amazing what treasures you can discover with a microscope!) all the way down to species—for example, our three species of wombat. Can you work out where you might fit in the family tree?

RED KANGAROO

KINGDOM:	Animalia
PHYLUM:	Chordata
CLASS:	Mammalia
INFRACLASS:	Marsupialia
ORDER:	Diprotodontia
FAMILY:	Macropodidae
GENUS:	*Macropus*
SUBGENUS:	*Osphranter*
SPECIES:	*Macropus rufus*

GOLDEN WATTLE

KINGDOM:	Plantae
CLADE:	Angiosperms
CLADE:	Eudicots
CLADE:	Rosids
ORDER:	Fabales
FAMILY:	Fabaceae
CLADE:	Mimosoideae
GENUS:	*Acacia*
SPECIES:	*Acacia pycnantha*

HUMAN

KINGDOM:	Animalia
PHYLUM:	Chordata
CLASS:	Mammalia
ORDER:	Primates
SUBORDER:	Haplorhini
INFRAORDER:	Simiiformes
FAMILY:	Hominidae
GENUS:	*Homo*
SPECIES:	*Homo sapiens*

EARLY CURIOSITIES

For Indigenous Australians, native animals were not at all odd or curious. They were simply part of their life and land for tens of thousands of years. Early rock art reveals beautifully crafted imagery of animals, revealing deep cultural and spiritual significance to Indigenous people. Animals were, and still are, a source of nutrition, tools and decoration. They also feature in ceremonies, dances and traditional stories that are passed down from generation to generation.

ROCK ART

Europeans would have marvelled at the abundance of sea turtles in Australian waters. Of the seven species of sea turtle in the word, six live in our waters. Turtles are important to many Indigenous people as a source of nourishment, and also because the shell was used to make combs and hooks. **An Indigenous name:** ngarlaa.

KOALA

Our cute and cuddly koala wasn't very well liked by early settlers. It was called a monkey, a bear, a sloth and 'a senseless torpid creature'. Its name comes from an Indigenous word meaning 'no drink'. **Some Indigenous names:** cola, colo, koolah, koolewong, yarri, kulla.

WOMBAT

The wombat was thought by Europeans to be a combination of a bear, a possum and a badger. British artist Rossetti described it as 'a joy, a triumph, a delight, a madness'. The name 'wombat' comes from the Dharug language. **Some Indigenous names:** wombat, wumbat, warreen.

KANGAROO

Quadrupedo chiamato *KANGUROO* ritrovato su la Costa della nuova Olanda.

Europeans were enchanted by the roo. Captain Cook described it as 'a light mouse colour and the full size of a greyhound'. Joseph Banks took one kangaroo and two wallaby specimens back to England. **Some Indigenous names:** kanguru, gangurru, bagaray, bamburr, woora, munthu, nunguu.

CASSOWARY

Cassowary of New South Wales.

The cassowary has long been prized by Indigenous people for food, decoration and tools. Early settlers likened the bird to the emu, and described it as delicious —'a better supper and breakfast than we had enjoyed for some months'. **Some Indigenous names:** gunduy, gundulu, goondoye.

PLATYPUS

Dubbed the 'water mole', the platypus stunned and confused settlers who thought it a combination of a duck, an otter and a beaver! It took scientists nearly 100 years to prove this mammal laid eggs. **Some Indigenous names:** mallangong, gayadar, tambreet, boonaburra.

For the first Europeans who landed on our shores, native animals were absolutely odd and curious. Many of our creatures both confused and delighted. A gumleaf-gobbling monkey with fluffy ears, no tail and a pouch? A furry egg-laying mammal with a beak and spines? A hopping greyhound with a pouch, paddle-like feet and an enormous tail? These paintings show early interpretations of our unique and curiously odd fauna.

SUPERB LYREBIRD

Because of this bird's incredible ability to mimic almost any sound, white settlers found its calls unsettling. When its feathers became prized in Europe, the bird's population around Sydney began dwindling. **Some Indigenous names:** bulln-bulln, weringerong, woorail.

ECHIDNA

Possibly the most curious native animal of all, zoologist George Shaw described it: 'Amongst the most curious and interesting of quadrupeds yet discovered'. **Some Indigenous names:** innar-linger, kulai, piggi-billa.

KOOKABURRA

Nature's alarm clock, the kookaburra's raucous laugh certainly alarmed European arrivals, describing it as 'a hideous chorus of fiendish laughter'. Its name is from the Wiradjuri word 'gugubarra'. **Some Indigenous names:** gugubarra, gugagaga, kho-khoo-kha-kha.

EMU

Settlers were amazed by the emu's tiny, useless wings and impressive size, dubbing it a super bird. Captain Arthur Phillip called it 'of the ostrich kind'. He sent one to England where it was stuffed and presented to Joseph Banks. **Some Indigenous names:** barrimal, murawung, birabayin.

CROCODILE

Imagine how terrifying crocodiles would have appeared to early settlers. Indigenous people collected and ate crocodile eggs, and would sometimes eat a small crocodile. **An Indigenous name:** pukpuk.

TASMANIAN DEVIL

Dubbed the 'zebra opossum', these savage creatures became the stuff of legend in Europe, and were soon rumoured to be man-eaters, born of the devil! Lieutenant-Governor William Paterson described the Tassie devil as 'the only powerful and terrific of the carnivorous and voracious tribe yet discovered on any part of New Holland'. **Some Indigenous names:** tarrabah, poirinnah.

FLYING FOX

Early explorers named the flying fox the 'vampire bat'. But they soon discovered that this curious flying mammal, with the body of a bat and the head of a fox, doesn't drink blood. It only eats fruit! **Some Indigenous names:** wuka, gundenwi.

INDEX BY ANIMAL GROUP

INDEX A – Z

GLOSSARY

AMPHIBIANS – ectothermic vertebrates with no scales, living on land and in water, including frogs, toads, salamanders and newts
APEX – at the top; an apex predator (e.g. crocodile) is at the top of the food chain
AQUATIC – living in water
ARACHNIDS – 8-legged invertebrates, including spiders, scorpions, ticks and mites
ARBOREAL – living in trees
ARID – dry
ARTHROPODS – invertebrates with an exoskeleton, a segmented body and pairs of jointed legs (e.g. ant)
BILATERAL SYMMETRY – an animal that can be divided only one way, into two halves that are a mirror image of each other
BINOMIAL NAME – scientific name (e.g. saltwater crocodile = *Crocodylus porosus*)
BIODIVERSITY – the variety of plant and animal life in a particular habitat
CARNIVORE – an animal that eats only meat
CARTILAGE – like soft, flexible bone (found in our noses and ears)
CLADE – a group of organisms that has an ancestor and all lineal descendants in common
CONSERVATION – protecting, preserving and restoring the natural environment
COURTSHIP – dating . . . before things get serious!
CREPUSCULAR – active at dawn and dusk
DIURNAL – active in the day
ECOLOGY – the balance of all living things and their environment
ECTOTHERMIC – partly heated by the environment (e.g. the sun), not just by body processes
EMBRYO – an unborn baby in the process of development
ENDANGERED – seriously at risk of extinction
ENDEMIC – native to a certain area or country
ENDOTHERMIC – body mainly heated by processes going on within the body
ERA – a long period of history
EXOSKELETON – a rigid external covering for certain invertebrates (e.g. scorpion)
EXTANT – existing, living
EXTINCT – no longer living
FOLIVORE – a herbivore that eats only leaves
FRUGIVORE – an animal that eats only fruit
GENUS – a taxonomic category that sits between family and species, e.g. kangaroos are in the *Macropus* genus
GONDWANA – the southern hemisphere supercontinent that contained Australia, New Zealand, South America, Africa, Arabia, Antarctica and the Indian subcontinent

HABITAT – the natural environment for a plant or animal
HERBIVORE – an animal that eats only vegetation
HIBERNATION – the time an animal spends in a dormant state, e.g. 'sleeping' through the winter
INSECTS – arthropods with an exoskeleton, a segmented body, antennae and three pairs of jointed legs
INVERTEBRATE – without a spinal column (e.g. snail, spider)
LAURASIA – the northern hemisphere supercontinent that contained North America, Greenland, Europe and Asia (excluding the Indian subcontinent)
MAMMALS – vertebrates that feed milk to their young, and are divided into three types—monotremes (e.g. platypus, echidna), marsupials (e.g. kangaroo, koala) and placentals (e.g. bat, whale)
MARSUPIALS – mammals that give birth to undeveloped young that mature in a pouch and suckle milk
MEGADIVERSE – including the majority of the world's species, and high numbers of native species
MEGAFAUNA – land animals at least 130 per cent larger than their modern equivalents, most often of the Pleistocene era, and becoming extinct within the last 40,000 years
MONOTREMES – mammals that lay eggs but also suckle their young
NOCTURNAL – active at night
OMNIVORE – an animal that eats both meat and plants
PANGAEA – a supercontinent that included all of earth's current landmasses and is believed to have broken apart (to form Laurasia and Gondwana) in the Mesozoic era
PHASMIDS – insects that eat leaves and resemble leaves or sticks
PLACENTALS – mammals that grow babies in a placenta and give birth to live young
PREDATORY – preying on and eating other animals
RADIAL SYMMETRY – animals that can be divided into many mirror image halves (e.g. jellyfish)
RANGE – the area in which a plant or animal is found (indicated in this book as 'HOME')
REPTILES – ectothermic vertebrates (including snakes, lizards, crocodiles and turtles) that typically have dry, scaly skin and lay soft-shelled waterproof eggs
SCAT – poop, droppings
SCLEROPHYLL – hard-leaved vegetation, e.g. eucalypts
SPHEROID – a sphere or ball that's not perfectly round
SUBSPECIES – different kinds of a single species, e.g. the western grey kangaroo (*Macropus fuliginosus*) has two subspecies—*Macropus fuliginosus fuliginosus* and *Macropus fuliginosus melanops*
SYMMETRY – one side being the mirror image of the other
TERRESTRIAL – living on land
TORPOR – a state of decreased activity that allows an animal to conserve energy
VERTEBRATE – with a spinal column (e.g. dog, dolphin)

ILLUSTRATION LIST

page 48

TURTLE ROCK ART

Parks Australia
Turtle and Barramundi, Nanguluwur Rock Art Site, Kakadu, 2014
photograph; 40.1 x 26.9 cm
courtesy Parks Australia

KOALA

Koala
(London: Wyman & Sons Ltd., 1880s)
coloured engraving; 12.8 x 19 cm
nla.cat-vn789540

WOMBAT

Choubard (engraver, active 1807–1830) after Charles Alexandre Lesueur (1778–1846), under the supervision of Jacques-Gérard Milbert (1766–1840)
Nouvelle-Hollande, Ile King, Le Wombat, 1807
hand-coloured engraving; 24 x 31.5 cm
nla.cat-vn1998223

KANGAROO

Filippo de Grado
Quadrupedo Chiamato Kanguroo Ritrovato su la Costa della Nuova Olanda, 1770s
engraving; 23 x 18.3 cm
nla.cat-vn2760953

CASSOWARY

Cassowary of New South Wales
(London: John Debrett, 1789)
engraving; 22.5 x 17.5 cm
nla.cat-vn375677

PLATYPUS

Edouard Traviés (1809–1865)
L'ornithorhynque, 1860s
colour lithograph; 25.1 x 17.1 cm
nla.cat-vn487610

page 49

SUPERB LYREBIRD

Sydenham Edwards (c.1769–1819)
Lyrebird, 1802
pen & watercolour; 41 x 32.2 cm
nla.cat-vn1379365

ECHIDNA

Echidnas and Emus, c.1880
chromolithograph; 17.6 x 26.3 cm
nla.cat-vn1498661

KOOKABURRA

George Raper (1769–1796)
Laughing Kookaburra (*Dacelo novaeguineae*), c.1788
watercolour; 40.7 x 32 cm
nla.cat-vn3579224

EMU

Vincent Woodthorpe (active 1794–c.1802)
Emu, 1802
hand-coloured engraving; 14.2 x 10.2 cm
nla.cat-vn623421

CROCODILE

Thomas Baines (1820–1875)
Alligator, Victoria River, Tom Tough Aground, c.1856
watercolour; 7.3 x 13 cm
nla.cat-vn2221698

FLYING FOX

John Gould (artist, 1804–1881) and Henry Constantine Richter (lithographer, 1821–1902)
Pteropus poliocephalus
plate 28 in *The Mammals of Australia, vol. 3*, by John Gould (London: John Gould, 1863)
nla.cat-vn760101

TASMANIAN DEVIL

John Gould (artist, 1804–1881) and Henry Constantine Richter (lithographer, 1821–1902)
Sarcophilus ursinus
plate in *The Mammals of Australia, vol. 2*, by John Gould (London: John Gould, 1863)
nla.cat-vn760101